D0064675

WILLARD SCOTT'S
DOWN HOME STORIES

By

Willard Scott

THE BOBBS-MERRILL COMPANY, INC.
Indianapolis/New York

Published by The Bobbs-Merrill Co., Inc.
Indianapolis/New York
Manufactured in the United States of America
First Printing
Designed by Jacques Chazaud

Library of Congress Cataloging in Publication Data

Scott, Willard.
Willard Scott's Down home stories.

1. Anecdotes—United States.   I. Title.
PN6261.S35   1984   818'.5402   84–11054
ISBN 0–672–52768–5

CONTENTS

ACKNOWLEDGMENTS

I hope those of you who read this book have even half the fun and laughter we all had working on it. The person who was in charge of the writing and shaping of the manuscript was my friend William Proctor. We spent many hours, mainly stuffing ourselves in New York City restaurants, putting this material together. Only the two of us know why our guffaws got all those stares from the staid patrons of one elite university club dining room.

I'm also grateful to Charles Langston, alias "Felton Cheekey," whose help in gathering and editing many of the stories was invaluable. Chuck used to write material for me and Eddie Walker when we were on the "Joy Boys" radio program in Washington D.C. Chuck, I hope you've made more money out of this book than you did from "Joy Boys!"

The nation's politicians, all of them my friends, have also made invaluable contributions to these pages. These members of Congress and governors of our great land have often given the American public a good belly laugh—in more ways than one. They know more than most that without a sense of humor, it's easy to be driven to tears or the bottle.

Finally, I appreciate the editorial and research help of Todd Moore and Janet Ernst in pulling the threads of this manuscript together.

Willard Scott

P.S. Special thanks are also in order to Bill Adler, who had the good sense to bring us all together and the even better sense to leave us alone while we worked.

WILLARD SCOTT'S
DOWN HOME STORIES

I

WHY HAPPINESS IS GOOD MEDICINE

As I reach each milestone of life—whether major or not so major—I always set aside time to sit back and take stock. It just so happens that I've recently passed two important ones: I've turned fifty years old and I now weigh 250 pounds. With half a century and an eighth of a ton under my belt, so to speak, I feel I have some rather weighty reasons to reflect on where I've been and to consider where I'm going.

As I think back on the events that have made up my life, it strikes me that I'm, by nature, a happy person. This pleases me to no end because the more people that I meet—and I meet many, from all walks of life as I travel about the country—the more I'm convinced that as long as I stay happy, I'll have a good shot at living another fifty years. And if I'm still in good health when I reach my hundredth birthday, that's okay by me.

Without getting too philosophical, I can say that my accomplishments in the working world aren't as important to me as some of the more basic things: I'm still *alive,* I'm still *working,* and I'm enjoying a good *home life* thanks to the grace of Almighty God. For what it's worth, I'd like to share some of the things that make me laugh and help me feel good.

There are lots of things that make me smile. For one thing, there are stories that I like to remember, those that describe funny, warm, universally human experiences. (After all, we're all in this together!) For that reason, I can rely on certain people to make me laugh. Buster Keaton, Fred Allen, Jack Benny, Abbott and Costello, Sid Caesar, and even such imaginary characters as The Muppets and Goofy have all earned a place in my heart by tickling my funnybone with their honest portrayals of human foibles and life's quirks.

There are also lots of people who have made me feel good just to watch them. It could be the cast of characters one night on "Grand Ol' Opry," or the comfortable smiles and gestures of such diverse personalities as Arthur Godfrey, Walter Cronkite, Bing Crosby, or Franklin Roosevelt. The presence of people like these and others just seems to give me a warm, comfortable feeling that makes me feel at home.

This is the key to happiness for me: *home.* Above all else in my life, being at home—or being in the midst of an environment or people who remind me of home—makes me feel good and secure. Nothing can beat the familiar details that add up to a feeling of home: sitting in front of a warm fire with a glass of "Jackie D."; having my wife, Mary, by my side; knowing that the kids are okay; and watching the dogs snoozing on their Bean beds nearby.

For me, there is something about a fireplace that makes things seem all right: a fireplace is a kind of centerpiece for happiness. My good neighbor Eddie Strother, a Virginian now ninety, once told me something that I've never forgotten. "A fire is like an old friend," he said. "It not only warms you and gives you light, but it *comforts* your spirit as well."

Like Eddie, I enjoy the comfort that a warm fire brings. For one thing, it offers me a peaceful feeling that is tough to match. Perhaps that's because I've become accustomed to using a fire for warmth as well as for the center of those quiet times spent with the family. For another thing, a flickering fire sparks my penchant for storytelling and reminiscing about life.

Sometimes when I'm staring into my own fire, I'll recall things I heard long ago, or lessons I learned from people like Eddie, who have lived decades longer than I have. That's why one of my favorite things to do on the "Today" show is to announce the birthdays of people who have reached the age of 100 or older. They are wellsprings of good, old-fashioned wisdom, with so much to tell us. Older folks give me a personal connection to the past and to the familiarity of home that strikes a chord within me.

My old friend Eddie recently let me in on one of his "down-home" pearls of gardening wisdom that I treasure. To save my surplus garden vegetables over the winter, he taught me how to dig a hole in my garden below the frost line and stuff it with straw. In this outdoor "root cellar"—courtesy of Mother Earth— I could keep my home-grown turnips, potatoes, and beets fresh all winter long. It really works, too. They're just as good and sweet in the spring as when you placed them there in October.

One time, I myself literally stumbled across one of these homespun nuggets, inadvertently discovering a remedy for the cold that had pestered me for days. Since I was on my farm, I trundled off—achey head, runny nose, and all—to be by myself in the springhouse—that's a kind of shed we built over a fresh-water spring on our property. Though I often visit the spring-house to get away from it all, this time I went there with a practical purpose: to try to ward off the cold by using some of the venerable folk remedies that had been around our family for generations.

Though my eyes were red and puffy, I found my "remedy"—a bottle of Jack Daniels left to chill in the cool spring—and took a hefty swig. I took a big chew of Beech-Nut tobacco and a swig of "Jack" and began to chew and savor the "therapeutic" juices. A tad more Jack Daniels was in order, so I helped myself once again to the bottle and started back toward the house, still sloshing the entire mess around in my mouth.

It was then that I accidentally added my own special touch to the remedy: I tripped and swallowed the whole slippery mouthful of chewing tobacco and whiskey.

I was sure I was going to die.

My ears started to ring, and I broke out in a cold sweat. Everything started to swim around me as I lay there on the hillside. But amazingly enough, those horrible, nauseous feelings passed in a couple of minutes. When it was all over, I realized all the cold symptoms had gone! No more achiness, scratchy eyes, or runny nose—I was cured!

Old folks like Eddie Strother and my grandmother have a lot to say about the secret of longevity. As I said, I've had the pleasure of meeting many of these senior citizens face-to-face because of my involvement in the "Today" show, and many are in remarkably good health. While their secret strategies to ensure long life often conflict, I collect them all. I like to keep my bases covered.

For instance, they may either attribute their longevity to not smoking, or to smoking a lot; to not drinking, or to drinking a lot, every day; to strong religious convictions, or to "free form" living.

Well, you can debate issues like these until Miami freezes over—particularly if you're of the "drink a lot, every day" school of thought—but I have found some qualities among the ageless that seem to be common to all. For one thing, these are people who can adapt to any situation. They've learned to "roll with the punches," or to make do with the cards that life has dealt them. In other words, somehow most of the centenarians I have talked with have learned how to handle their anxieties effectively.

Most important of all, at the very center of this marvelous ability to adapt is invariably an enduring sense of humor. They possess the ability to laugh at the world, and at themselves—a skill that surely must be one of the greatest relief valves known to the human race. Somebody once said, and I don't quite know who, or if I'm quoting exactly, "You can't argue or get mad or fight with anyone when you're laughing." For me, that's the bottom line.

I've got to count among my greatest blessings my willingness to laugh at life. I've been blessed with, so say my ex-teachers, an overabundant sense of humor. It's served me well as my cushion against the tragedies and challenges of life. Luckily, a sense of humor is a relief valve natural to each of us, whether we are 10 or 110. While it's physically possible, though not probable, to reach the age of 110 without laughing all the way, those who do are the special people who, at 110, are still young at heart.

The type of humor that I love the most is not necessarily the typical joke with a punch line. My preference is for those funny, offbeat anecdotes about significant human experiences—the quips, sayings, and down-home stories that can teach us something about our shared fallibilities.

To put it another way, the best stories are often those that make a point. For instance, my old friend Henry Greene told me about his neighbor, John, who just couldn't get the engine in his tractor tuned to perfection. Not only that, the more John fooled around with the engine, the more he seemed to mess things up.

One day, when Henry was paying John a visit, he decided to take a look at the tractor himself. After a brief inspection, he asked, "John, just how old is that tractor?"

"Oh, it's got to be about twenty-five years, I guess," John said.

"Twenty-five years and it's still running? John, if it ain't broke, don't fix it!"

Some of my favorite stories, including a number that teach

equally helpful lessons, have been told to me by the nation's politicians who collectively bring a cross-section of down-home American humor to the nation's capital. I've lived in or near Washington D.C. most of my life so I've always been in touch with a lot of these political figures. I can tell you that many elected officials come to Washington still acutely aware of the down-to-earth roots of their own humble beginnings; and as a result, they have a strong awareness of what is going on in the United States at the grass-roots level. Their favorite stories reflect the kind of humor and wisdom that enhance the most profound kind of happiness in life.

These politicos instinctively know the truth expressed by one of my favorite philosophers, Ralph Waldo Emerson, who wrote: "To laugh often and much: . . . this is to have succeeded." But they also know that the power of humor can enrich one's life far beyond the capabilities of material success. The capacity to step back and smile can transform sick minds and bodies into havens of blooming health.

There's no doubt about it: Happiness *is* good medicine for all our ills. I don't know about you, but when my spirits are high, I feel like my blood flows more freely. My whole body begins to feel good. In fact, good humor energizes me, so that I feel like a real dynamo throughout the entire day.

What's even more important, good humor is the only medicine I know that can be infectious. If you try to see the good humor in a bad situation, well, it's like pulling the fat out of a fire. Bad situations can get transformed into beautiful ones. Also, you can defuse an awful lot of arguments with a kind word. So now, I want to invite you to enjoy with me some of the stories that have helped to put a shine on my day.

II

PORK BARREL

feel lucky to have had a lifetime of opportunities to see history in the making—even though some history, once made, isn't so hot. When I was just a kid, my family, which at the time lived in Virginia, packed into the bus one afternoon to see Franklin Roosevelt inaugurated. Soon after Pearl Harbor had been attacked, I visited the capital and saw what looked to be rows of antiaircraft guns mounted right on top of the federal buildings. Years later, I found out they really didn't have guns up there at all. They were only wooden models some politician with a psychological bent provided to give us some peace of mind and a sense of security. It always serves to remind me that political beauty is only skin deep. To get to the heart of the matter you might do well to bring along a pick and shovel.

I still have a great interest in our nation's politicians—some are pure show biz, others are people of great energy and compassion, but they're all subject to the "applause meter" of public opinion. As I said earlier, I've always felt there is a natural affinity between politicians and other public personalities and celebrities. We're all hams at heart, whether gristly or tender, too salty, too dry, or even only half-baked.

A lot of responsibility goes into maintaining a public image. As a result, politicians' and celebrities' activities are both very carefully scrutinized. Although I'm sure that I've been forgiven a lot of gaffes that people just wouldn't accept from their elected representatives, I do get some flak from people, just the same. While working as a weatherman in the Washington D.C. area, I went into a polling place during an election to vote. Standing outside shaking hands with voters, was Joel Broyhill, the congressman from the district, who was also my choice candidate.

"Joel," I said as I shook his hand. "I have a good feeling about this, and I want you to know that I predict you're going to win this election."

"Willard," he said quickly, "I appreciate your good wishes, but I've seen your weather predictions. Please don't predict I'll win, or sure enough, I'm going to lose."

Lincoln's Wit

Many successful politicians have found that a good sense of humor can be invaluable. I like to think that finding areas of mutual agreement is what politics is all about. To bring together opposing points of view, it helps to have a person who can keep everything in perspective—one who can add a light touch to even the most serious of occasions. We've had quite a few yarn spinners in our halls of Congress, and even a good number in the White House. Abraham Lincoln, one of my great heroes, was known for telling stories with a punch.

To counter a charge that he had made some errors in judgment, Lincoln once told a story about a lawyer and a minister who were arguing.

As they rode down the road together, the minister said, "Sir, do you ever make mistakes while in court?"

"Very rarely," the lawyer sniffed, "but on occasion, I must admit that I do."

"And what do you do when you make a mistake?" asked the minister.

"Why, if they are large mistakes, I mend them. If they are small, I let them go. Tell me, don't you ever make mistakes while preaching?"

"Of course," said the preacher. "And I dispose of them in the same way that you do. Not long ago, I meant to tell the congregation that the devil was the father of liars, but I made a mistake and said the father of *lawyers*. The mistake was so small that I let it go."

If Looks Could Kill

Another story I like to tell about Lincoln concerns the fact that he was never known to be a handsome man. In fact, he was regarded by many to be as homely as a mud fence, though not nearly as dense. Although he acknowledged this, he never thought his appearance was so bad as to cause people problems. One day, however, a man stopped him on the street and pulled out a gun.

"What seems to be the matter?" Lincoln asked the man calmly.

The man drew his eyes into a squint, and scowled, "I promised myself that if I ever came across an uglier man than myself I'd shoot him on the spot."

"Well, then, go ahead and shoot," Lincoln responded. "If I *am* uglier than you, I don't want to live!"

Horace the Mule

It's important for people in office—or running for office—to remember that their success in politics depends upon how competent they are thought to be. Perhaps my favorite tale of all time—one that I heard long ago and chuckle over at least once a year, around Election Day—concerns the fact that a public figure can't let down his guard for a minute. The real hero of this yarn is a single-minded fellow by the name of Horace the Mule.

"Doctor," Debra Sue said on the phone, "my mule Horace is sick, and I wish you would come and take a look at him."

"Oh, Debra Sue," Dr. Slater said, "it's after six o'clock and I'm eating supper. Give him a dose of mineral oil, and if he isn't all right in the morning, phone me, and I'll come and take a look at him."

"How'll I give it to him?" she inquired.

"Through a funnel."

"But he might bite me," she protested.

"Oh, Debra Sue, you're a farm woman and you know about these things. Give it to him through the other end."

So Debra Sue went out to the barn to tend to poor Horace. He held his head low, and he moaned and groaned like Debra Sue had never heard before.

She looked around the barn for a funnel but the closest thing she could find was her Uncle Bill's fox-hunting horn hanging on the wall. It was a beautiful gold-plated instrument with gold tassels hanging from it.

So, Debra Sue took the horn and affixed it properly to the mule's backside. Horace paid no attention, being too sick to care at this point.

Then, she reached up on the shelf where medicines for the farm animals were kept. But instead of picking up the mineral oil, she picked up a bottle of turpentine—and she proceeded to pour a liberal dose of it down into the horn.

Horace raised his head with a sudden jerk, his eyes blazing. He let out a hoot that could surely have been heard a mile away. First rearing up on his hind legs, and then bringing his front legs down with a crash, he knocked out the side of the barn, jumped a five-foot fence, and started down the road at a mad gallop.

In excruciating pain, Horace tried and tried to eject that horn as he ran down the road, but without success. All that he was able to do was make that horn blow every few jumps he took.

The dogs in the neighborhood knew that when that horn was blowing, it meant one thing: Uncle Bill was going fox hunting. So out on the highway they charged toward the sound, following close behind Horace.

It had to have been the most unusual sight anybody in that county had ever seen. First, there was Horace—running at top speed, the hunting horn in a most peculiar position, with mellow notes tooting, the tassels waving. The dogs brought up the rear, barking joyously behind him.

This arresting spectacle passed by the home of Old Man Ben Jacobs, who was sitting on his front porch. He hadn't drawn a sober breath in fifteen years, and he gazed in fascinated amazement at the vision that unfolded before his eyes. Understandably, he couldn't believe what he was seeing. Some people say that this incident is what finally drove Old Ben to become head man for Alcoholics Anonymous in the southern section of the state.

By this time it was getting dark. Horace and the dogs were approaching the river, and the bridge tender heard the horn blowing. He figured that a boat was approaching, so he hurriedly went out and opened the bridge. Horace went overboard and was never heard from again. The dogs also went off the deep end, but they swam out without very much difficulty.

It so happened that the bridge tender was at that time running for the office of county sheriff. But, because of this incident, he managed to poll only seven votes.

After all, the people figured, any man who didn't know the difference between a mule with a horn up his rear and a boat coming down the river wasn't fit to hold any public office in the county.

Life Sentence

Being in the public eye has its drawbacks, to be sure. For one thing, the press sometimes can misinterpret what a public figure is saying—and that can lead to problems. Just as an editorial writer can criticize a political candidate, television critics can also have their way with personalities on the tube. It's always open season on celebrities, and when you're in the public eye the only way to deal with it is to develop a thick skin and a ready sense of humor.

It's happened to me, and it's also happened to Governor Allen I. Olson, of North Dakota, who was formerly *attorney general* of that state.

He told me about one constituent who was well known to Olson's staff when he was attorney general because he absolutely murdered the English language, much in the tradition of Casey

14

Stengel. His most notorious mistake was that he would always ask to speak to the *"Eternal General."*

In one speech, Olson jokingly referred to him as the attorney general's number-one supporter because he thought Olson would be in office forever.

The press, apparently, either didn't get the point or just lacked a sense of humor. The next day, Olson picked up one of the daily papers and saw a column criticizing the arrogant young attorney general who thought he could be attorney general as long as he wanted!

Mug Shot

Being on television, I see firsthand how the split-second timing of a public production can produce slip-ups. Usually these mistakes are very trivial and are easily glossed over. But sometimes they present more of a problem.

During the final days of his 1984 Republican primary campaign for governor of North Carolina, Congressman Jim Martin received an urgent phone call in Washington from an aide in Raleigh, the state's capital. A local television station, the aide said, had telecast a report about a sexual assault trial in which the defendant was someone else surnamed Martin. As the anchorman read his report, a photograph of Congressman Martin was shown on the screen.

After explaining the error the aide asked: "What do you want me to do about it?"

"First," replied Congressman Martin, "I think you should call and tell them I'm innocent."

Beg Your Pardon

Most politicians that I've met work hard for their constituents. They truly enjoy the opportunity to do things for people, and they maintain busy district offices just for that purpose. But sometimes, they come across requests that stump them.

Oregon's Governor Vic Atiyeh picked up the phone once to find an Oregonian calling from California. The man told Atiyeh he faced charges in California and said he wanted to be extradited back to Oregon.

The governor, of course, realized that it wasn't so simple. So he told the constituent, "Well, in order to be extradited, you would have to have committed a crime in Oregon."

"Oh," said the caller. "What crime would you like me to commit?"

True Politician

In years past, open range policy was often a highly controversial issue in the South and Southwest, especially in rural areas where there was an abundance of livestock. Under open range policy, horses, cows, and other farm animals were turned loose to graze on public lands. Since these public lands included the grassy sides of roads and highways, the policy sometimes resulted in collisions between a cow and a car, or a mule and a car. Nonetheless, open ranges were given up only in recent years, mainly in the South.

At one political rally I attended, a local politician was running for public office in an area that included one of these rural districts where the open range was still recognized, though hotly disputed. The candidate's aides had recommended that he support it since open range advocates were in the majority. The politician said, "Leave it to me." And that's exactly what they did.

When it came time for him to speak, the politician got up and gave a fervent and enthusiastic endorsement to open range policy. He said that it had been a guiding light and a moral force in his family for unnumbered generations. Moreover, he declared, it would remain so for generations yet unborn. He did everything but recommend a constitutional amendment to assure the sanctity of open range, thundering, "I will stake the whole of my political future on it." Then, he paused dramatically, and added by way of conclusion: "Now, let's get these damn cows off the highway before somebody gets killed!"

Republican Visitor

My trips out to the far reaches of the country often find me spending the night in some small place far off the beaten path. In the Northeast, I like to stay at inns with some history behind them. You know, those that all seem to claim "George Washington slept here."

If that's true, then he was one president who sure got around.

In the South, of course, the little hotels have their own local luminaries they can point to as former visitors. During a recent political to-do I attended in Georgia, another visitor stopped at the only hotel in town with vacancies and asked for a room for the night.

"I'll give you the best one in the house," the clerk said. "William Jennings Bryan once slept there."

The visitor, being a Republican, smiled weakly and went up to his room. When he opened the door, he was astonished to see a couple of rats scurry into the corners of the room. He went immediately back to the desk to change his room.

"But sir," the clerk protested, "there's nothing at all wrong with that room. In fact, that's the same room that William Jennings Bryan slept in."

"I know, I know, and William Jennings Bryan is bad enough," the man responded. "But I surely don't intend to sleep with the entire Democratic party!"

Lone Star Washington

I'm constantly astonished at the way historians dig up new versions of history, or find some shred of evidence that puts a new light on a point in our past. But their discoveries can't hold a candle to some information Senator John Tower of Texas passed on to me. He said that he's found some startling evidence about the father of our country:

"Very few people know that George Washington actually was a Texan. When he was a young boy, he chopped down his father's favorite mesquite tree with his new hatchet. His father returned from a hard day of riding the range and demanded to know who had cut down his prized tree.

" 'Father,' young George said, 'I cannot tell a lie. I chopped it down with my Bowie knife.'

" 'Son,' his father replied, 'we're moving to Virginia. With an attitude like that, you'll never make it in Texas politics!' "

Worse Than Death

Although he is a member of the United States Senate, one of the world's most dignified and venerable bodies, Senator Gordon Humphrey of New Hampshire has managed to maintain his sense of balance. He isn't bedazzled by power or position, as the following observation by the senator clearly illustrates:

"Nothing is certain in life but death and taxes. But at least death doesn't get worse every time Congress convenes."

Promises, Promises

Although the Book of Proverbs in the Bible is one of my favorite sources of wisdom, I've discovered a few similarly wise sayings that have sprung up in our own day. For example, Senator Jeremiah Denton of Alabama is a political conservative who summed up part of his philosophy of politics for me in the following observation:

"You know, I've heard it said that there are three phrases that should always put you on your guard. One is 'Honey, I love you and I'm leaving my wife.'

"The second is, "The check is in the mail.'

"And the third is, 'I'm from the government, and I'm here to help you.' "

Time's Up

In Missouri, they apparently know how to keep their politicians in line, as this story I heard recently from Bill Emerson, who represents that state's 8th Congressional District, goes to show.

"A certain candidate for political office in rural Missouri once spoke for well more than his allotted five minutes at a county gathering. One gentleman in the crowd was especially irritated by the candidate's lack of courtesy and respect for the other candidates. So, in Missouri, where the pioneer spirit is still prevalent, he pulled a pistol from inside his coat and shot the candidate on the spot.

"Now, Missourians are, of course, honest, law-abiding citizens, so the man immediately got in his pickup truck and drove to the county sheriff's office to turn himself in.

"Upon entering the sheriff's office, he told the deputy that he had just shot a candidate for office and was prepared to suffer the consequences. But the deputy merely told him that he was in the wrong part of the courthouse.

" 'What do you mean I'm in the wrong part of the courthouse?' asked the offender. 'I just shot a politician.'

" 'Yes, I know,' replied the deputy. 'The game warden's office is down the hall, and that's where you go to collect your bounty.' "

Modesty Prevails

When Henry Kissinger was secretary of state, his ego was the subject of a lot of good-natured wit and humor. It was said, for instance, that if Kissinger had grown big enough to fit his ego, he would have been fifteen feet tall. When Senator Pete Wilson of California was mayor of San Diego, he had the pleasure of introducing Secretary Kissinger at a cocktail party in Southern California. It was well past the cocktail hour, and perhaps that explained the fervor of his remarks.

Wilson said, "If they were alive today, Talleyrand, Prince Metternich, and Cardinal Wolsey would be taking lessons from Henry Kissinger."

Dr. Kissinger calmly came to the microphone, cleared his throat, and said, "Mr. Mayor, your introduction is one with which no rational person could disagree."

Landslide Waterloo

In December of 1936, Alf Landon was a guest speaker before Washington's famed Gridiron Club. This was shortly after he had lost the presidential election to Roosevelt. The governor carried only two states: Maine and Vermont. In his remarks, as he made reference to that contest, Governor Landon confirmed for me the fact that a little humor is the best path to perspective on even our most devastating problems.

"A friend of mine wrote me recently that he doubted if my political experience had prepared me for the result of this election. I replied that he didn't know us Jayhawkers. If there is one state that prepares a man for anything, it is Kansas.

"The Kansas Tornado is an old story, but let me tell you of one. It swept away first the barn, then the outbuildings. Then it picked up the dwelling and scattered it all over the landscape. Both the farmer and his wife were knocked unconscious.

"As the funnel-shaped cloud went twisting its way out of sight, leaving nothing but splinters behind, the wife came to, to find her husband laughing. She angrily asked him, 'What are you laughing at, you darned old fool?'

"And the husband replied, 'The completeness of it.' "

Art of Compromise

The Reagan philosophy of cutting back funding for high-spending social programs has been a continual target for the Democrats. Senator John Glenn of Ohio said at one point that the administration now appears ready to compromise, but in its own way:

"The Administration has taken its lumps on Social Security. Even their own commission couldn't decide whether to make the retirement age sixty-five or sixty-eight. So I hear they have compromised. Under their new plan, Social Security will *start* at sixty-five—and *stop* at sixty-eight."

Bush-Whacked

Vice-presidents of the United States are seldom taken very seriously. This is essentially because officially they have virtually nothing to do. Under the Constitution, they preside over the Senate and assume the presidency should that become necessary. And that's all. But sometimes, future vice-presidents get a little preparation for not being taken seriously. This experience, related to me by Vice-President George Bush, reminds me of some of my own slights as a fledgling newscaster:

"When I was first running for public office—for the United States Senate in 1963—I was campaigning in east Texas, desperately trying to find places to speak.

"A very small GOP county convention was being held at a school, after their Halloween fair. Only a handful of people were in the room for our scheduled eight p.m. meeting. At five past eight, one or two people were drifting in. I was all fired up to give my big pitch for primary support.

"The co-chairman spoke up and said, 'What *I* have to say is *important,* so while the others are still coming in, I would like to introduce George Bush of Houston.' "

Career Change

As a great football fan, I've always counted as one of my gridiron heroes Representative Jack Kemp of New York, who was a quarterback for the Buffalo Bills before he entered Congress. Unfortunately, his last season on the team was a disaster, and upon announcing his retirement, he said he was thinking of running for Congress. But the way things were going for him at the time, he wasn't counting too heavily on his success.

"If I throw my hat into the ring," Kemp said, "you can bet that it will be intercepted."

Letter Perfect

It's hard enough for me to keep up with my own mail, but at least I don't have to cope with the demands and requests many politicians get. With all the letters that pour into congressional offices each day, it's a wonder that any of them get read at all.

But most congressmen tell me that they absolutely *do* read and pay attention to their mail. It has to take priority because, after all, letters are the voice of their constituents. A personal letter from a neighbor back home can tell a lot more about what's on people's minds than the most sophisticated polls.

On a bad day, however, all you get is criticism.

Representative Andy Jacobs, Jr., told me that one such bad day, he received a letter addressed to the "Honorable Andrew Jacobs." The note went on to say, "I use the term 'honorable' to address you merely out of respect for your office. . . ." After heaping abuse on the congressman, the letter closed, "William F. Snard IV."

Congressman Jacobs quickly made a reply: "Dear Mr. Snard IV: I use the term 'IV' to address you merely to point out that you may be in violation of one of your own Virginia State statutes. Perhaps you recall the famous case of Buck vs. Bell (274 U.S. 200) in which the Supreme Court in passing on a Virginia Sterilization Statute held, in the opinion of Mr. Justice Holmes, 'Three generations of imbeciles are enough.' "

Name Calling

That must have been really a bad day for our revered representative because later that same day Congressman Jacobs received yet another unflattering tidbit: "Dear Mr. Jacobs: You are an incompetent jerk. Sincerely, Lem Smith."

Jacobs was moved to respond: "Dear Mr. Smith: Thank you for the kind compliment. Naturally I should dread being competent at being a jerk. Sincerely, Andy Jacobs, Jr. P.S.: Just in case you didn't intend to compliment me, you, sir, are an incompetent name caller."

Long Winded

I've been told I have received an excessive dose of the gift of gab, but I'm in good company. Plenty of public figures have earned a reputation for giving unnecessarily long-winded speeches. My friend Senator Jennings Randolph of West Virginia recalls that it was his wife who first pointed out the dimensions of his mouth problem.

"Back in the mid-1930s, I gave a campaign speech at a small town named Harman, near my home in Elkins, West Virginia. I felt that although lengthy, the speech was well received. Driving back home late at night, I asked Mrs. Randolph for her reaction. 'Mary, how did the speech go?' I inquired. 'Very well,' she replied, 'except that you missed several excellent opportunities to sit down.' "

No Effort is Wasted

As you probably know, everything begins and ends in the television business with knowing and influencing your audience. The performer's career depends largely upon his personal audience ratings and those of his show.

Understanding your audience is also critical to a political campaign, as Senator Jennings Randolph discovered on his first campaign in 1930. On one occasion, he walked through the apple orchards of Jefferson County in the eastern panhandle of West Virginia. While there, he chatted with the pickers and packers in the long rows of apple trees, greeting those on long ladders in treetops. Also, he walked for hours in what seemed like a "fruitful" campaign swing.

Late in the day, one of the workers approached, and, with pleasant concern, said, "Mr. Randolph, we are glad to have you visit us, but I should tell you that you are asking for our votes while you are at least a half-mile over the border in Virginia. We can't vote for you!"

The candidate was shocked at the news, but he managed to recover with a typical politician's reply:

"Yes, I know that. But you and your fellow workers have friends and workers over in West Virginia who *can* vote."

Incumbency Blues

In television, the longer your show runs, the more you have to do to keep up audience interest. But in politics, the opposite seems true: The longer you're in office, the less you have to do to keep your job. So there's a widely held belief in Congress that during an election campaign, the incumbent holds a terrific advantage. After all, his name is already a household word in his district, and he has the ability to command immediate attention in the press.

Sometimes, though, as Senator Bob Kasten of Wisconsin found out, being the officeholder doesn't always count for much.

As he campaigned for reelection in his hometown of Thiensville, a young man rushed over to say how pleased he was to meet Kasten. "I'm so glad that you're running for Congress," he said. "The guy we have up there now is a real jerk!"

Junket Reward

Every job has the potential for a boondoggle, or unauthorized trip or activity that benefits the individual rather than the organization. People are always asking me, "Hey, Willard, when are you going to get a real job? You just travel where you want and joke around all day with the folks, don't you?" Well, that's not quite true, but I have come in for my share of criticism.

Some officeholders have been criticized for abusing the trips—or junkets—that they are allowed to take on behalf of the government. In fact, many people often suspect that they are just thinly disguised vacations.

One suspicious reporter once asked Representative Frank Horton of New York if he, too, was considering going off on any of these junkets.

To the reporter's surprise, Horton admitted that he was.

"First I'll be going to Phoenix, then Mexico," he said, as the reporter scribbled furiously, "then I'm off to Rome, and then Verona. I'll also be going to Pulaski, but I'll have to go through Texas to get there."

"And this is all on government business?" the reporter probed.

"I'll say it is," Horton shot back. "They're all towns in my district, and I'm having office hours."

Bullfrog Upset

Representative Wes Watkins of Oklahoma says that in his state, campaigning often gets personal, and sometimes the most effective campaign tactic can be to hold the opposition up to ridicule.

Many years ago, Watkins told me, Charley Flanagan, who was the representative from his Cotton County district in 1937, was later defeated by a man named Thomas Huff. During the time that Tom Huff was in office, he had voted for a bill that prohibited the taking of bullfrogs from a local river.

Then, when Charley Flanagan challenged Huff once again in the next election, Charley made a speech that people still talk about to this day:

"All Tom Huff did in the past two years is vote for the bullfrogs . . . and they weren't even Cotton County bullfrogs. You know, as night falls, you think those bullfrogs are saying 'knee-deep, knee-deep, knee-deep.' Well, let me tell you, my friends, they ain't singing that; they are singing 'Tom-huff, tom-huff, tom-huff.' "

Charley Flanagan was reelected to his old seat, replacing the friend of the bullfrogs.

The Sheriff

A man named Vance, who lived in Virginia, ran for sheriff a few years back. But he was soundly beaten, getting just five hundred votes out of five thousand cast. Shortly after the election, a mutual friend of ours saw him coming down the street, a revolver strapped around his waist.

"Hey, Vance, I thought you lost," my friend said. "What are you doing packing that pistol?"

"Listen," Vance said grimly, "a man with no more friends than I've got in this town had better carry a gun."

Kennedy's Clubs

In the early days of the Kennedy administration, the press paid a lot of attention to the clubs the young president belonged to. They wanted to know, for instance, what the qualifications for membership were. Did they select—or exclude—prospective members on the basis of race, creed, or color?

A reporter friend of mine in Washington was making these inquiries, and he was determined to ferret out the details. But most private clubs are very close mouthed about their membership policies, so finding this information was difficult, if not impossible.

After many frustrating attempts at several clubs, the reporter finally put in a call to the Ancient Order of Hibernians. His call was answered by a man with more than just a trace of an Irish accent.

"What are the qualifications," the reporter asked, "for membership in the order?"

"Well, I'll tell you, son," the man replied, "it helps if you're an Irish Catholic."

Patriotic Couple

Senator Bob Dole of Kansas has long been a person I've admired, and he's certainly a notable public figure on his own accord. But once his wife Elizabeth was named President Reagan's transportation secretary, the Doles gained newfound notoriety.

"I feel a little bit like Nathan Hale," Senator Dole said after his wife's confirmation. "I regret that I have but one wife to give for my country."

Strange Bedfellows

Sometimes people have trouble imagining someone in the public eye shaving in the morning, brushing teeth, blowing out wet hair, and wiping the sleep out of the eyes. But believe me, my Mary and I go through these routines every morning (though I don't worry too much about my hair). It's the same way with most politicians I know.

After Elizabeth Dole's Cabinet appointment, a magazine showed a photo of Senator Bob Dole at home, helping the secretary make the bed. The senator immediately got an irate letter from a guy in California who said the senator should never allow a picture to be taken of a man doing such things around the house. The guy was particularly upset, apparently, because now *his* wife was making him help with the housework.

Senator Dole, however, was unmoved. "Look buddy," Senator Dole responded, "you don't know the half of it. The only reason she was helping is because they were taking pictures."

On the Air

Verbal bloopers can really make me laugh, especially when they're on national television broadcasts. It's embarrassing enough when you flub up in front of a small group. But announcers on television—and especially, political reporters—are supposed to be totally smooth and professional. They take themselves very seriously and try not to let anything ruffle their feathers. So, when they *do* make a mistake, the gaffe is magnified a hundredfold, because they are such serious folk and millions of people hear the screw-up.

I've had some experiences like this myself, but most of them were before my days in television. I was doing radio commercials years ago, and I did one for a soap product. Their slogan was, "for the skin you love to touch." Well, I read out, loud and clear, "for the *sin* you love to touch." It probably boosted sales 1000 percent.

A colleague of mine, a network television political correspondent in Washington, *always* had trouble when he had to refer to President Ford and Jimmy Carter in the same sentence. Invariably, he would say, in his most serious political reporter's voice, "President Ford and Jimmy Farter . . ."

Presidential Pit Stop

That correspondent was bad enough, but his blooper was topped by another newscaster I used to work with, who was announcing a local outing by President Eisenhower to "look" at his farm. But, "look" got garbled: "President Eisenhower today motored to Gettysburg," he said in serious tones, "where he took a leak at his farm for the first time in two weeks."

Unusual Cold Front

We must have been quite a crew, as I now think about it. On another newscast, a weatherman with the station apparently forgot his eyeglasses. His copy was as plain as day: "A huge cold air mass is sweeping across the Canadian border. . . ."

Instead, when he read the darned thing, it came out: "A huge cold mare's ass is sweeping across the Canadian border. . . ." Now that's what I call a meteorological disturbance.

Russian Defector

Worst of all, however, was the newscaster's flub when chronicling the flight of Svetlana Alliluyeva, Stalin's daughter, to the United States from Russia some twenty years ago. It was big news at the time, but the announcer just tripped over his own words: "Here is a bulletin from the Channel Four newsroom—Svetlana Alliluyeva, the daughter of Josef Stalin, has just defecated to the West."

African Visit

A politician went to Africa to visit various tribes, and everywhere he went, he gave a speech about how great a people they were, and what a mighty nation they had. He went on and on about how the American government was interested in their welfare. Each time he finished a sentence, he was extremely gratified to hear the natives cheer, "Hoopee, hoopee, hoopee."

After the speech, he waved to the crowd of natives and was euphoric at the success of his talk. "We really won them over, didn't we?" he said to an aide as he walked away, with cheers of "hoopee!" coming at them from all sides.

As he left, the village chief came up to him to shake his hand. "You be careful now when you go out into the jungle," the chief said. "It's still very wild . . ."

As the politician turned to leave, the chief added, ". . . and don't step in any buffalo hoopee."

A Political Animal?

Senator Bob Dole of Kansas always likes a good political battle, but even he was amazed at the latest crowd of Democratic Presidential candidates.

"Fact is," he said when the Democratic primaries were just kicking off, "there are too darned many candidates cluttering up the Democratic Presidential picture. You could cut the list in half by compressing two candidates into one. Like: Glenn and Mondale could be fused into 'Glen-dale.' McGovern and Hart into 'McHart.' Hollings and Cranston could be 'Holl-ston.' But then, there's Jackson and Askew. . . ."

Slow Motion

One of the most colorful of our governors, Edwin Edward of Louisiana, in a recent bid for office referred to his opponent as being so slow that it took him an hour and a half to watch "60 Minutes."

Adios from Adlai

Adlai Stevenson, former Governor of Illinois, was one of the sharpest wits our nation has produced. For example, at the peak of the Rev. Norman Vincent Peale's popularity, the governor was asked to compare Peale to Saint Paul. Stevenson replied, "I find Paul appealing—but Peale appalling."

He also knew how to reach back into the past and pick just the right words for any occasion. Perhaps the most difficult situations he faced were the loss of the Presidential elections to Dwight Eisenhower in 1952 and 1956. But after each of those losses, he showed his class. I can still remember getting choked up when he quoted Lincoln to one disappointed group of supporters: "I'm too old to cry, but it hurts too much to laugh."

III

OLD-TIME RELIGION

hen I'm in church, I always like to put my best foot forward. So, I tend to "tone down" a bit from my usual gregarious self. But try as I may to maintain a low profile, sometimes something happens that invariably draws attention to me. My mouth has gotten me into more hot water than anything else in my career, so I guess it only seems fitting for it to have given me problems in my religion.

One time when I was a kid, the congregation was receiving Communion in our local Baptist church. They passed the bread around and followed it with the "wine," which really was just a tiny glass of grape juice.

Everybody was supposed to take the bread and juice together, according to the tradition of our church, so I waited until everybody else started to tip their glasses. Then, I really went at it! I stuck my tongue right down into the little glass to get every last drop.

Unfortunately, the suction that formed between my tongue and the glass was so strong that I couldn't pull the glass loose! Hoping not to make a scene, I struggled to get that glass off without breaking it, but without success.

Then, as the congregation burst into song, I knew the acid test had come. If I didn't join in this final hymn, I'd raise a few eyebrows. So I finally came to a solution that was pure "Willard": I went right ahead and sang with that shot glass still wedged in my mouth.

Miraculously, when the song was over, the glass just popped out. I've heard that the Lord works in mysterious ways, but this was ridiculous!

When the Founding Fathers included freedom of religion in the Bill of Rights, who would have suspected the variety of churches that would spring up in the years that followed? There seem to be as many different denominations and separate congregations as there are ways to express that basic American need for independence.

The fledgling churches and spiritual movements became an integral part of America's developing culture. In fact, in areas more than a stone's throw from the major cities, where manmade laws were often hard to enforce, the rules and customs of local churches would often control social conduct. There was real power in that kind of grass-roots religion. Naturally, colorful folk stories about religious faith and practice cropped up nearly as quickly as the new sects in this spiritually fertile soil— tales and anecdotes about our heritage that you won't find in history books.

Here's one truly inspired little story that continues to renew the faith of a special breed of modern man often tried by fire.

Trial by Fire

A man knocked at the Heavenly Gate, his face was scarred and
old.
He stood before the man of fate and asked admission to the fold.
"What have you done," Saint Peter asked, "to gain admission
here?"
"I've been battling government bureaucracies," he said, "for
many and many a year."
The Pearly Gates swung open wide, and Saint Peter touched the
bell,
"Come in and choose your harp," he said. "You've had your share
of hell."

Town Rivalry

Sometimes regions or cities develop a kind of competitive rivalry
like the one fostered and enjoyed between St. Paul and Minneapolis, Minnesota. St. Paul struck the first blow, establishing
itself as the first big city in the vicinity. Though it maintained its
dominance for quite a while, Minneapolis recently not only
caught up but has become the major city in the area, relegating
St. Paul to the shadows. Still, a mayor of St. Paul was quick to
point out one obvious advantage bestowed upon his city by the
Almighty Himself. "You can read the Bible from cover to cover,"
he said, "but you'll never find the word 'Minneapolis.' "

Wise Words

- If your shirt is separated from your pants, so that the skin shows in between, denizens of the Deep South have a spiritual explanation: They say "Your body is separated from your soul!"

- Thought for chronic backsliders and lukewarm believers in general: "Today we are liable to fall, tomorrow up we climb, for 't ain't our nature to enjoy religion all the time."

The Baptism

Just about everyone must have some dirty deeds in their past they'd like washed away and down home in the South where I grew up, a lot of folks were very particular about just how to do the washing. When I was a kid—though it's still true today—people would really get up in arms about the way a person ought to be baptized. The Methodists thought a little sprinkle of water on the head was sufficient. Then, there were those, like all your Southern Baptists, who felt that only a thorough dunking would do the trick.

In fact, many of the fundamentalist preachers liked to do their baptizing in a real river, just as Jesus was baptized.

Whatever the method, it's a serious event in a believer's life, and I'd be the last one to poke fun at it. But as for the people who were getting baptized, well, they were often quite a cast of characters. Some of the things that happened on those occasions could lighten up even the most solemn moments.

For example, I've heard that there once was a young lady who lived her life in what we would call the fast lane. At the urging of the town's priest, she finally repented of her sins in life, and then she went to be baptized in a small river on the outskirts of town.

"Now, Veronica," the priest said, "I'm going to wash all your sins away."

"My goodness," giggled Veronica. "*All* of them—in that little itty bitty ol' creek?"

Liars

One church revival service reached a high point when Sam, a notorious liar, was finally converted. Although it was the middle of winter, the minister decided to baptize the penitent prevaricator on the spot before the man had a chance to reconsider.

The temperature was so low that the ice had to be broken in the creek, but they went ahead with the ceremony anyway. When it came time, the liar was immersed in the frigid water, and then he waded ashore.

"Was the water too cold, Sam?" a deacon inquired, as the convert stepped out onto the bank.

"Oh no," Sam replied, "not bad at all."

"Dunk him again, preacher!" the deacon called. "He's still lying."

Speechless

Of course, as spiritual as we Americans are, we're also independent minded. So not everybody takes to the practice of baptizing by a dunking in the river. One time an old preacher was trying to baptize a big, fat woman but she wouldn't—or couldn't—bend her knees. Wanting to keep with the tradition of his church, the preacher was intent on going ahead and giving her a thorough dunking.

As he tried to get her down under the water the preacher yelled, "Do you believe?"

She grunted and groaned, but made no answer.

Struggling, the preacher managed to get the woman down a little lower. "Do you believe?" he repeated louder.

The woman grunted and groaned some more, but still gave no answer.

Finally, the preacher plunged the woman under the water, and as she came back up the preacher yelled once again, "Do you believe?"

"Believe?" the woman sputtered. "Sure I believe. I believe you're trying to drown me!"

The Fire Buzzard

Many baptismal ceremonies take place after revival meetings. An evangelist given to the old-fashioned, fire-and-brimstone style of preaching might rouse the crowd to such a furious pitch that the air seemed to crackle with excitement. Even the ordinary things that happened—like a door blowing open, or a loud sound—took on a new light. They were often interpreted by the electrified crowd to be direct messages from heaven. You can imagine what would happen when something truly unusual, yet purely coincidental, occurs.

One old fella told me that he remembers one such time when things got a little out of hand.

"It was a Saturday morning," he began in his Deep South dialect, "and Momma and Papa was going into town. They was going in the wagon with the mules and said they would be gone all day—wouldn't get back before dark, likely. They told me and my next oldest brother, Ermine, not to set the place on fire, nor run off none of the stock. Then, they pulled out for town.

"They wasn't out of sight, hardly, before Ermine crawled up under the porch where there was a goose setting on some eggs. He wanted to see how many eggs was under her, he said. But you know how a goose is. They can be as mean as sin, especially one that's trying to hatch eggs. So when Ermine got under the porch, that goose come off her nest and near whupped the hell out of him with her wings before he could back out. 'Course that made him mad and nothing would do but he must get even.

"Back then, we had an old cur dog around the place—'Blue,' we called him. Well, Ermine set Blue on the goose and what does that fool dog do but kill her! We knowed we would catch it good and plenty when Momma and Papa got back from town for sure now. We had to do something, so we taken the goose down in the back of the field and throwed it in a stump hole. We should of covered it up, but we didn't think of that. We was just kids, you know—a couple of big, overgrown boys. So, all we done was throw some leaves in on top of it. 'Course the buzzards found it right away and commenced to circle. Now what does Ermine do but decide we ought to catch us a buzzard. So we done it. It ain't hard. Once they light, they're slow and clumsy.

"What we done was—now this'll tickle you—what we done was, we taken a piece of grass rope about three feet long and soaked it in some coal oil. Ermine fastened one end of the rope to a piece of baling wire, and hooked the other end of the wire around the buzzard's leg. Then we set fire to the rope and turned the buzzard loose to see what it would do.

"Well there was a brush arbor set up about a mile down the road, and inside there was a revival meeting going on. It was just starting to get dark and folks was starting to holler and yell like they do when the preacher gets going. Now what does that fool buzzard do but make straight for that brush arbor with that piece of burning rope trailing out behind him. About then, somebody at that meeting looked up and seen that piece of rope. 'Course it was too dark by then to see the buzzard.

"I wasn't there, but they tell me you never heard such a carrying on in your life. Wimmen and childrun was screaming. Two or three of 'em fainted, they said. Some of the men broke for the woods, some of the others tried to get their teams unhitched. But with all the racket, their mules and horses was bucking around, and some of 'em actually run off.

"Ever'body taken that piece of burning rope in the sky to be a sign from heaven. A sign of what, they didn't know. They must of been a hell of a lot of sinning going on over there, because I judge they didn't take it to be a sign of nothing good.

"About then, the preacher hollered for ever'body to get inside because they wasn't no better or safer place to be at such a time, what with the wrath of the Lord falling in on 'em, and all. So ever'body done it. They was still crying and wailing and carrying on, and the preacher, he was doing his best to comfort 'em when that fool buzzard managed to shake off that piece of burning rope, or it just come aloose. Anyhow, that brush arbor had been there for a week and a half, and it was dry as tinder. And when that piece of rope fell on it, it flared up like a pine knot, and all them sinners come pouring out again.

"This time, they wasn't no stopping 'em. That broke up the meeting for good and all. Some of 'em run off and left their wagons and didn't come back for 'em until late the next day.

"Momma and Papa got home about then. They said you could see the fire for five miles. Folks was still streaming by our place, and 'course they all had a story to tell, and no two of 'em the same. The preacher, he said it was a sign from the Lord that somebody better get right. Me and Ermine knowed better, but we knowed better than to dispute a preacher, too, so we said nothing.

"Anyhow that buzzard saved our skins, me and Ermine's. Momma figured all the commotion scared the goose so bad it run off. So it turned out, we didn't get a whupping after all."

That story really captures some of the flavor of the small, rural communities that I remember as a child. They were places where people took it for granted that the extraordinary things that sometimes happened were miracles from heaven. Not every occurrence was supposed to have a logical explanation. Now, I for one do believe that real miracles occur every day of our existence. But at the same time, there are miracles . . . and there are miracles.

A Miracle of Convenience

A sweet, little old lady was returning from a trip to Ireland and was going through customs at Kennedy Airport in New York.

"Do you have anything to declare?" the customs agent asked.

"No, nothing," the sweet woman replied.

"What's this, then?" the agent said, pulling out a bottle of pale, amber liquid from underneath a Bible in her suitcase.

"Just a bottle of water from the blessed River Shannon," she said.

The skeptical agent unscrewed the cap and sniffed the contents. Then, he took a small sip. "River Shannon water my eye!" he said. "This is Irish whiskey!"

"Glory be to God!" the little old lady exclaimed with her hands held in the air. "A miracle!"

Dead Duck

Speaking of well-timed miracles, some people seem to go to any lengths to prove they're right.

One duck hunter was loudly bragging about his skill in a local tavern one day when he said something that the others just couldn't let pass.

"Why," he said, "if I ever missed one of those dang birds, I sure don't remember it."

The listeners decided to put the old hunter to the test, and they convinced him to meet them the next morning in a duck blind. So when the next day dawned, the first rays of the sun found them sitting quietly over the water awaiting their prey. Sure enough, a duck soon came into view, and the old hunter whispered, "Sit tight. I'll show you what it's like to never miss."

With that, he blasted away. But the duck flew on.

Looking at his nearest challenger, the hunter widened his eyes. "Well, son," he said, "you're witnessing a miracle. Yonder goes a dead duck—flying."

Strange Spirits

Although they may be everybody's idea of high moral living, our friends in the clergy are as human as the rest of us. I myself have a lot of respect for the clergy and I wouldn't want anyone to think otherwise. But they face the same kinds of problems and embarrassing moments in their day-to-day lives that we do.

For example, one young minister fresh from divinity school was assigned to a secluded church in the country to assist an older minister who was preparing to retire.

44

Things worked out well enough, but the younger man had a problem with his nerves. Frequently, during a sermon, he would get very tense and jittery, and his nervousness presently began to affect the impact of his message.

When he confided in the older minister about his difficulty, the elder man confessed surprisingly that he, too, had had the same problem at one time. But he also had a method for dealing with it.

"Have you seen that little glass of water I always take up to the lectern with me?" the older man asked.

"Why, yes, I have," the young fellow said.

"Well, that's not water," the older minister whispered. "It's gin. And every time I start to feel nervous and jittery, I sip a little of that gin, and it calms me right down."

The young minister thanked him profusely, and said he would certainly try the gin method. After his sermon the following Sunday, he asked the minister for an evaluation.

"You made a few mistakes," the older man said slowly. "I said use a *little* water glass. You had a tumbler. I also said to take *little* sips, and you were knocking back some pretty big swallows. Those are relatively minor mistakes and not really important.

"But your third mistake *was* important," he continued, "because I don't believe Daniel kicked the hell out of that den of lions."

Forgetful Preacher

Another young minister was about to deliver his first sermon. He had chosen as his text the eleventh verse of the third chapter of Revelations, wherein the Lord says, "Behold, I come quickly."

Intending to inject a bit of drama into his sermon and get the attention of his congregation, he gripped the edges of the lectern and said with great feeling, "Behold, I come quickly." But at that instant, his mind went totally blank, and he could not remember a word of what he had planned to say next.

Fighting down panic, and hoping to jog his memory, he repeated, even more emphatically, "Behold, I come quickly." But once again, he couldn't remember the next line. Except for that phrase, his mind remained blank.

Reduced to emergency measures now, he stepped down to the edge of the rostrum, seized the railing in one hand, gave it a vigorous shake and thundered, "Behold, I come quickly!" But the railing gave way, and he tumbled right into the lap of a little old lady seated in the front pew. Filled with embarrassment, he scrambled to his feet and managed an apology.

"It's all right, young man," the little old lady replied calmly. "I've got nobody to blame but myself. You warned me three times and I just sat there."

Running Off at the Mouth

We've all been in situations where we've heard something that was particularly eloquent, and we've said, "I wish I'd said that."

Well, I've got the opposite problem. I don't know how many times I've said to myself, "Gee, I wish I hadn't said that." That's when I say or do something that I know I'll regret later, that is, if I don't regret it immediately. Sometimes, there's real value in keeping your opinions to yourself. But one thing's for sure: I know I'm not alone.

A woman boarded a bus in a little hamlet in North Carolina and immediately started chattering. She seemed to have a comment on everything and everybody the bus passed. For a while, her remarks were entertaining. But as she continued without letup for mile after mile, her talkativeness started to wear on the other passengers. Still, she gave no sign of running down.

Late in the afternoon, the bus stopped at a little town in Georgia, and a young man stepped up in the door to get several parcels from the driver.

Before he could step back off the bus, the woman called out to him, "Say mister, what town is this? This must be the most godforsaken looking place I've ever seen."

The young man grinned at her and replied gently, "Oh, it's not so godforsaken, ma'am. Stick around and go to church with me Sunday, and I'll show you."

Before the woman could think of a suitable comeback, the man had stepped off the bus and was gone. "Who was that snippy young fellow?" she asked the driver.

The driver chuckled. "That's the Baptist preacher in this town, lady."

Noah's Choice

Sometimes, believe it or not, I've found myself at an utter loss for words. To guard against this speechless condition when something totally unexpected happens, I just try to keep as "light" and flexible in my mind as possible, so as not to let anything throw me. I have the greatest respect for people who naturally "think on their feet," or who have cultivated the verbal comeback skills to redeem themselves from sticky situations.

For instance, there was an old preacher once who told some boys of the Bible lesson he was going to read in the morning.

The boys, finding the place, decided to play a prank and tore out some of the key pages.

The next morning the preacher began to read to the congregation from his selected passage. "When Noah was one hundred and twenty years old he took unto himself a wife who was . . ." and then going to the next page, continued, ". . . one hundred and forty cubits long, forty cubits wide, built of gopher wood, and covered with pitch inside and out." Puzzled, he checked it again to see if he had read it correctly the first time.

"My friends," he said after a pause, "this is the first time I ever read this in the Bible. But I accept it as evidence of the scriptural assertion that we are 'fearfully and wonderfully made.' "

Well-Read Parishioners

A minister started his service one Sunday morning by announcing that his text was taken from the 41st chapter of Matthew.

"How many of you have read this chapter?" he asked his parishioners.

Hands shot up all over the auditorium.

"You're the ones I want to talk to, then," said the minister, "because there is no such chapter."

Vegetable Garden

For people of the cloth, sermonizing isn't just a Sunday affair. But sometimes, they seem to reach a little too hard for a message.

A rather pompous Episcopal minister was out walking one day and he came alongside a beautiful vegetable garden where a member of his congregation was working. Just a few months before, the spot had been a veritable jungle of thorns, weeds, and tree stumps. "My goodness, Josh," the minister exclaimed. "You and God certainly have made a beautiful place here." Josh straightened up slowly, wiped the sweat from his brow, and answered, "You should have seen the mess this place was in when God had it by Himself."

Perfect Timing

I have to admit that I don't find every visit to my church to be an exciting time. In fact, there have been days when I couldn't wait for the service to be over. Unfortunately, it seems the preacher always picks those days for a particularly lengthy lesson. At times like that, I've thought that someone forgot to give him the "cut" signal.

There was one preacher I heard of who used to time his sermons by sucking on a mint. As he began, he would reach into his pocket and stick a mint into his mouth. When the mint was dissolved, he knew it was time to wind down his sermon.

One Sunday, though, he reached into his pocket, pulled out a button and stuck it into his mouth. Sure enough, at three o'clock in the afternoon he was still going strong!

Stamps

There has always been a considerable amount of competition between the various Christian denominations. I guess folks in each denomination think that they know the best route to heaven, but there are so many different views that sometimes it's easy to get confused and straddle the fence.

A meek little man in this position went into the post office to buy some stamps.

"How many?" barked the postal clerk.

"I'd like a hundred," said the little man.

"Okay," said the clerk. "What denomination?"

The little man looked nervously over his shoulder, then replied timidly, "I guess you'd better give me fifty Episcopal and fifty Catholic."

Paths to Heaven

Each denomination has its own claims to superiority; and I'm not sure that's all bad. I suppose, if you're going to become a true believer and develop a set of convictions that will really change your life, you have to choose a straight and narrow road in life. But is it possible to go overboard? Consider this interchange*:

After his doctrinal sermon, an Episcopal bishop was asked, "Is there a way to get to heaven other than through the Episcopal Church?"

"Yes," said the bishop, "there are other ways, but no gentleman would take them."

---

* From *Native American Humor* by Walter Blair (New York: American Book Co., 1937), pp. 449–51.

Whistle Stop

There's no doubt that some degree of competiton exists among denominations. I guess each one has its own personality. The diversity of beliefs may say more about us as a people than about the "right" way to believe on fine theological points.

Once, a railroad brakeman walked onto a train, sat on the seat opposite to me, and announced, "I went to church yesterday."

"Yes?" I said. "And what church did you attend?"

"Which do you guess?" he asked.

"Some Union Mission church?" I hazarded.

"Naw," he said. "I don't like to run on those branch roads very much. I don't often go to church, and when I do, I want to run on a main line, where your run is regular and you go on a scheduled time and don't have to wait on connections."

"Episcopal?" I guessed.

"Limited express," he said. "All parlor cars and two dollars extra for a seat. Fast time, and it stops at all the big stations—it's a nice line but it's too expensive for an express train."

"Universalist?"

"Broad gauge," said the brakeman. "Does too much complimentary business. Everybody travels on a pass. The train orders are rather vague, though, and the trainmen don't get along well with the passengers."

"Presbyterian?" I persisted.

"Narrow gauge," he continued. "A pretty track, straight as a rule, a tunnel going right through the mountain rather than around it. Spirit level ungenerous, the passengers have to show their tickets before they can get on the train. It's a mighty strict road. The cars are a little narrow so's you have to sit straight in your seat and there's no room in the aisle to dance. But you don't hear of an accident on that road, it's run right up to the rules."

"Maybe you've joined the Freethinkers?" I said.

"Scrub road," he scoffed. "A dirt roadbed and no ties. No

time card and no dispatcher. All trains run wild and every engineer uses his own time just as he pleases. Smoke if you want to, a kind of go-as-you-please road. Now, you see, sir, I'm a railroad man and I don't care to run on a road that has no time, makes no connections, or runs nowhere, and has no superintendent. It may be all right for some, but I railroaded too long to understand it."

"Did you try the Methodist Church?" I asked.

"Now you're shouting," he said enthusiastically. "Nice road, eh? Fast time and plenty of passengers. Engineers carry a power of steam and don't you forget it, steam gauge shows a hundred and enough all the time. Lively road, when the conductor shouts, 'All aboard!' you can hear him to the next station. Pretty safe road, but I didn't ride over it yesterday."

"Then maybe you went to the Congregational Church," I ventured.

"Popular road," said the brakeman. "An old dirt road, too— one of the oldest in the country. Good roadbed and comfortable cars. Well-managed road, too, directors don't interfere with division superintendent's train orders. Always has such a splendid class of passengers."

"Perhaps you tried the Baptist?" I guessed once more.

"Aha!" said the brakeman. "She's a daisy, ain't she? River road, beautiful curves, sweeps around everything to keep close to the river. But it's all solid ground and rock bed, single track all the way and side track from the roundhouse and the terminus. Takes a heap of water to run it though, double tanks at every station, and there isn't an engine in the shops that can pull a pound or run a mile with less than two gauges. But it runs through a lovely country. Those river roads always do. Yessir, I'll take the river road every turn for a lovely trip, sure connections and good timing, no dust blowing in at the windows."

But just here the long whistle from the engine announced we were pulling into the station. The brakeman hurried to the door as the conductor shouted, "Zionsville!"

An Irish Blessing

Instead of just saying "Good luck," I sometimes like to rely on the poetic spirit of the Irish to deliver a sendoff to friends or loved ones:

> May the road rise up to meet you,
> May the wind be always at your back,
> May the sun shine warm upon your face,
> And rains fall soft upon your fields;
> And until we meet again,
> May God hold you in the hollow of His hand.

Another favorite of mine: "May your soul be in heaven a half an hour before the devil knows you're dead." Also, I like this: "I hope you live *forever* and that mine is the last voice you hear."

Long-Lost Father

It's interesting the ideas people have of what heaven is going to be like: pearly gates and marble mansions, angels with wings all flying around and playing harps. That's okay, but not quite my style. I like to think that heaven is going to be a place where I'm going to feel the same way I do down in my old springhouse on my farm, kind of peaceful and serene. There'll be lots of good folks to visit and swap stories and share laughter with. I expect heaven to be a joyous place, and it wouldn't surprise me to hear a story like this when I approach the Promised Land:

As Jesus walked past the Pearly Gates one morning, Saint

Peter asked him if he would mind the Celestial Entrance for a few minutes while he ran a few errands.

"You know the routine," Saint Peter said. "If anybody shows up, just get the basic facts for the Book of Life."

Jesus told him not to worry, and Saint Peter scampered off to his errands.

Soon, a very old man with a flowing white beard arrived, and asked for admission.

"Fine," said Jesus. "Just let me get some information for the Book of Life. Now, what was your occupation on Earth?"

"I was a carpenter," the old man replied.

Jesus nodded approvingly and made a note of the answer. "Family?" he asked.

"I had just one son," the old man replied softly. "But I lost him a long time ago."

Jesus stopped writing and looked up. Could it be? There was a definite physical resemblance—and the family information . . . it was uncanny. He had to ask. "Father?" he said at last.

Startled, the old man peered at him closely. "Pinocchio?"

IV

ANIMAL CRACKERS

ike millions of other Americans, I love animals. Families everywhere may harbor their own special menageries of birds, goldfish, snakes, hamsters, or gerbils. But as I said earlier, one of the moments that I treasure most is when I can sit in peace with my dogs at my feet. They've got to be my favorite animals, because they really do have their own individual personalities.

If you spend enough time with a dog, you kind of get to know what's on his mind. A dog's face is so expressive, you can tell if he's exuberant, frustrated, or just plain contented. I suppose that's why I have three of them: Leslie, a retriever; Chumly, a Bassett hound; and Blackie, a mixed breed.

Now Chumly is kind of a strange dog, mostly because he

doesn't have the greatest disposition. One minute he'll be lying next to me with his head on my leg, but as soon as I have to move, he'll growl and snap at me. That's rather a disconcerting habit for a dog who likes to snuggle up on a master's lap. I've heard that it comes from too much in-breeding or something like that, but we never noticed it when he was just a puppy.

When he was about six months old, however, we took him to the beach and everybody gathered around to see the cute little Bassett puppy. One lady picked him up and started to coo into his face, and Chumly got so upset that he bit her! (See where flattery gets you?) Ever since then, he's been a little weird, as ready to snap as to snuggle.

We've tried everything to calm him down, even to the point of taking the advice of one vet who told us to have him neutered. Though the logic didn't sit quite right with me—after all, if someone neutered me, I'd be even meaner!—I reluctantly agreed. Sure enough, Chumly *did* get meaner. But we'd never get rid of him. We've just learned to accept our crazy dog, like we accept our crazy friends and relatives; and we love him in spite of himself.

To tell you the truth, I'm somewhat suspicious of people who don't like animals. I would rather deal with animal lovers, because that tends to say something about their compassion for other things. One of Solomon's proverbs suggests that you can tell the character of a man by the way he treats his animals: "A righteous man cares for the needs of his animal, but the kindest acts of the wicked are cruel" (Prov. 12:10). Some righteous people may also be busy people—it can take time and effort to be righteous—so they limit themselves to birds or goldfish, but I've built up flocks of furry and feathered friends to keep me company.

In addition to my three dogs, we must have fourteen barn cats back on the farm. I say "barn cats" because they're really half wild. They're not the sort of animals you give free run of the house to. Instead, these are strays that have wandered onto the property and then signed on for the long hitch. They just make themselves at home in a pile of hay in the barn, and spend the rest of their time mousing or catnapping.

I know some people can't stand stray cats, and maybe it's because they tend to multiply like rabbits. We had one tomcat we used to call the All-American, because he made seventy-five yards a night! As active as he was, we finally had to have him fixed. Now I don't know who ever dreamed up the word "fixed." It's probably the only time that fixing something means making sure it'll never work again. Anyway, that poor old tom spent the rest of his days perched on top of the bread box, just staring. He was probably dreaming of the good ol' days.

Fixing our male cats was my wife's answer to the cat over-population problem. Talk about a female chauvinist; I guess it never occurred to her to have the female cats spayed, too. When the cats kept multiplying anyway, it finally dawned on us that word had probably gotten out in catdom what fate befell male cats who wandered near Willard's farm. So the females apparently decided to take matters into their own paws. Instead of waiting for the tomcats to sneak in, the fertile females went on the prowl themselves to seek mates. After a few more litters of kittens, my wife finally relented and had the females spayed as well.

Though recently we've tended to concentrate on dogs and cats at the Scott homestead, I used to be in the chicken business. I had about 130 laying chickens. The problem is that chickens don't make the most companionable of pets. All they seem to care about is whether they have enough feed.

There have been a couple of hens that developed certain personalities of their own. When I would go out to feed them, the whole bunch would jump for the food. After a while, I noticed that there was always a couple of regulars who would hang around and wait for their heads to be stroked before they re-joined their feathered friends. But they were unusual.

Maybe that's why I like dogs so much. All they ask for is a bit of food and a little loving and they're your friends forever. Pretty soon, you can communicate with them just by a certain look, or a gesture of the hand. Not only do they seem to know what's on your mind; they have so much love to offer as well.

We have some other animals—a burro named Roberto and a horse named Tony. For me, it has been a joy to take care of the animals—from feeding the horse to tending to the chickens—and watching them grow stronger and healthier beside my growing children. Even the smell of the barn—the manure, the hay, the feed—makes me feel like a part of the natural process. I guess you could say that I feel a nurturing kinship with these animals, because it just makes me feel good to be with them, to take care of them, and have them care for me in return.

Byrd's Bird

Barn animals aren't everyone's style, I know. But that doesn't mean you have to shut yourself off from the pleasure of sharing a little love and good feeling with animal friends. Even in the hallowed halls of our nation's capital, there are a few political friends of mine who keep beastly company.

Senator Robert Byrd, for instance, is always on the phone talking with constituents back home or movers and shakers all over the country. In the past few months, however, one person I know complained about a strange tapping sound during his conversation with the senator.

Well, the phone isn't tapped, it's just Bruce—Senator Byrd's bird. This pet parakeet loves to alight on the senator's shoulder as he talks on the phone and peck away at the mouthpiece. Meanwhile, the caller gets two Byrds for the price of one.

The Prodigal Cow

During a break from his duties in the House, Congressman Dan Glickman of Kansas related one of his favorite stories—one that says a bit about the unpredictable nature of animals, and even more about the shrewdness of some of my good old country friends.

A farmer Glickman knew once kept a prize cow in a pasture through which a railroad track ran. Each day at exactly the same time, a freight train came through the pasture. One day, after the train had gone, the farmer discovered that his cow was missing. He promptly sued the railroad.

The railroad hired a brand new lawyer and just before the case came to trial, the young attorney bargained with the farmer, getting him to settle for half of what he had originally sued the railroad. Feeling very proud of his achievement, the lawyer just couldn't help bragging some.

"You know," he told the farmer as he handed over the settlement check, "you really had me worried. I didn't have any witnesses. The engineer was asleep and the brakeman was drunk. You could have won the whole amount."

"Well, young fella," the farmer said as he folded up the check and walked away. "You had me worried too. You see, that damn cow came home this morning."

Say It Ain't Sow

It may give me good feelings when I see some farm animals like cows. But whenever I see a hog, I wince a little. I just can't forget the time I was over at a friend's farm in Stanton, Virginia. They had this old boar hog that was an absolute winner at what we refer to as servicing—or romancing—the sows.

This one time, however, the boar was romancing a new prize sow, and he backed right into the electric fence and got zapped with 110 volts! Not only did that shock him out of the mood for that day, but from what I hear, he wouldn't go near a sow ever again.

From there on out, the only thing he was ever good for was rooting truffles.

Getting Her Gander Up

In rural towns, it's not unusual to see farm animals being transported around. But even country folk draw the line at allowing an animal inside a store. It's enough to make some people downright rude. I guess that explains an incident my cousin once told me.

A drifter walked into a bar with a goose tucked under his arm. A drunk looked him up and down, bleary-eyed, and said, "Where are you going with that pig?"

"That's not a pig, stupid," the man snapped. "It's a goose."

"I know that," the drunk replied indignantly. "I was talking to the goose!"

Horse Sense

A man with a goose in a saloon may be unusual. But soon thereafter, a horse cantered up to the bar and ordered a martini, very dry.

"A wise guy," said the bartender to himself, but he fixed the martini anyway.

"Bartender," said the horse as he sipped the drink, "this is an excellent martini. I think I'll have another one."

The bartender complied and the horse sipped the second one, pausing now and then to praise it also. He finished it and sat the glass down. "If you'll bring my bill," he said to the bartender, "I'll settle up now."

Seething at what he took to be a crude practical joke, the bartender said, "That'll be eighteen dollars and fifty cents."

"For two martinis?" the horse asked, a little incredulously.

"Eighteen dollars and fifty cents," the bartender repeated grimly.

With a sigh, the horse produced a leather change purse, opened it daintily with his teeth, and took out a twenty dollar bill.

The bartender was then convinced that he was dealing with a real horse, and that he was not being made the butt of a joke. So he said amiably, as he laid the horse's change on the bar, "You know, we don't get many horses in here."

To which the horse replied, "At these prices, I'm not surprised."

Penguin Outing

One bird lover I heard about from San Diego began to collect more and more exotic species. Finally, a traffic cop decided she had gone too far. He stopped her because she had six penguins riding in the back of her station wagon. "Lady," he said, "you can't drive around with those penguins in your car. Take those poor birds to the zoo."

The next day, he stopped the same woman again. The penguins were still in her car, but this time they were wearing sunglasses.

"Lady," said the police officer severely. "I told you yesterday to take those penguins to the zoo."

"Oh, I did," she answered brightly. "But today they want to go to the beach."

Got His Goat

Some of my forebears come from North Carolina, where there's a story that still goes around about a special kind of goat.

A man was driving along a country road when his engine suddenly quit. He got out and looked under the hood, but couldn't see anything wrong. Then, he heard a voice say, "You've got a bad generator."

He looked around, but the only other sign of life was a goat, chewing his cud, and watching from a pasture across the road. Thinking he must have just imagined hearing a voice, the motorist turned and peered under the hood again. And once again he heard a voice say, "You've got a bad generator."

He looked around again, but as before, the only other living being in sight was the goat. Truly frightened now, the man picked up his heels and ran.

About a mile down the road, he came to a gas station, where he related his adventure to the owner.

"Was this a brown goat, with a white patch on his back, and one crooked horn?"

"That's him, all right," said the motorist.

"Aw, don't pay him any attention," said the owner. "That goat is a good enough on body and fender work, but he doesn't know the first thing about engine trouble."

Bargain

Out in the country, people trade and buy livestock, much in the same way that city folks buy provisions for themselves in the supermarket. As in the city, a farmer sometimes comes across a deal he can't refuse. My old boyhood friend Fred tells this story about an experience he had to prove the point.

"I tell you what I'm going to do," said Fred to his friend Louis. "For a hundred dollars, I'm going to get you an elephant. What do you think about that?"

"I think it sounds crazy," Louis replied. "I don't want an elephant. I don't even like elephants."

"Don't be so stubborn," said Fred. "This is a deal I'm offering you; a full-grown elephant for just one hundred dollars."

"But I don't want a full-grown elephant for no hundred dollars," Louis protested. "For one thing, where would I keep it? And the mess they make. No sir. Count me out. An elephant I do not need."

"Tell you what I'll do," said Fred, eyeing his friend closely. "For a hundred and fifty dollars, I'll get you two elephants!"

"Now you're talking sense," said Louis.

Weather Lore

One of the things that I love about folk wisdom is the way country people can put diverse natural occurrences together and come up with some sage advice about the present or predictions about the future. The activities of wild animals, for instance, are taken in many places to be an important indicator of the coming weather. The more I ponder these points, the more I think I should do my weather reports for the "Today" show out in the woods, where nature may give better clues about what's going to happen than modern radar. Here are a few observations about animals and the weather that I've heard country friends repeat:*

- Signs of a long, tough winter: Skunks come in early from the woods and get under the barns. The coats of the foxes grow especially full. Walnuts fall by the bushel.

- Rain on the way: The hens "curl up and start picking."

- The end of the second quarter of the moon usually marks a definite change in the weather.

- If the storms of March are followed immediately by warm weather, it will be warm for the next six months, or at least there will be an early spring.

- If the last three days of January or June or August or any other month are rainy, the next month will likely be too rainy for much outdoor work.

- Cobwebs on the morning grass mean a clear pleasant day.

Along the New England coast, in particular, residents have

---

* Many of these are summarized in B. A. Botkin, ed., *A Treasury of New England Folklore,* revised edition (New York: Bonanza Books).

created their own methods for predicting a change in the weather. Some tell me these weather signals are, at best, good for conversation. But others see them as sure signs from nature that something, as they say, is "a-brewin'."

In the Boston area, for instance, there was "Old Solitaire," a one-legged gull who lived in the harbor for years. Yet it was rumored that when a person saw that gull before going out to sea, he could expect a hard blow ahead.

Around Provincetown, the inhabitants of that fishing community believed that gulls flying high over the harbor warned of a storm coming within a matter of hours. To confirm this "prophecy," people had only to look across the water at the Truro shore. If "the land looms high," people said, "you have another sure sign of heavy weather."

I must be missing out on something, judging by my record with long-term weather predictions. Apparently, even the shellfish know something that I don't—and with uncanny precision.

"When the oysters bed deep at Wellfleet," local wisdom says, "there will be a hard winter, and Provincetown Harbor will fill up with pack ice in February—floes so wide there won't be enough open water for a duck to light on, and so thick only the flatfish can navigate below."

Or try this: "If a chicken's gizzard comes away easily from the inner skin, look for an 'open winter'; and if a school of herring is raised in January, stow your overcoat for another year—especially if the ducks start laying ahead of schedule and the willows on the swamp banks bud too soon."

Finally, even insects and creatures of the night have something to say:

- Ants—Bustle and activity in the anthills: a sign of rain.

- Bats—Flying around late in the evening, in spring and autumn, means a clear tomorrow.

- Bees—When they stay in their hives, or fly only short distances, it will soon rain.

Cows in the Clouds

There was an old bit of weather lore that I first found out on that farm that had to do with the cows in the field. According to local legend, if all the cows are standing, it's going to be fair weather for the rest of the day. On the other hand, if the cows are all lying down, then you could bet it was going to rain in the next few hours. No one ever told me what it meant when half the cows were standing and half were lying down, however. I guess that means it's going to be partly "cowdy."

Circus Act

When I used to visit Grandfather Phillips' farm in Maryland for the summer, I learned a lot about animals and their habits. I especially used to love to climb on the backs of the cows because I knew I'd get an interesting reaction. They would "moo" and lumber off in their effort to get rid of me. That was all fairly tame sport until one day I climbed on the back of one dozing cow and it took off quicker than greased lightning. I went flying off to the side, and only later did I find out that I had tangled with my grandfather's best bull!

A donkey that allowed a lion to pull a similar riding trick was the star of a popular act in a traveling circus that occasionally came to our part of the South. But that donkey had a different experience than I did on the bull. You see, the donkey had been trained to let the lion jump onto its back and ride around the cage.

"That's really a spectacular act," a man said to the trainer. "Tell me, do they ever have a falling out?"

"Oh, they have their little disagreements now and then," the trainer confessed. "But when that happens, I just buy another donkey."

Pair of Canaries

I don't have birds as pets myself, but some friends of mine just love the way they sing, chirp, and talk. I've heard from bird-loving acquaintances that choosing a good singer takes a bit of skill.

When he first decided to buy his wife a canary, my friend went into a pet store to have a look around. His attention was immediately arrested by a little bird that chirped and trilled enthusiastically.

"I'll take this one," the man said to the clerk.

"Okay," said the clerk, "but if you take that one, you have to take the one in the next cage, too."

Now, the canary in the next cage looked terrible. Its beak was chipped, its eyes were red and runny. It had several bald spots where feathers were missing.

"But I don't want that awful-looking bird," the man protested, "I just want that one that's singing so nicely."

"Well, if you want that canary, you have to take the one in the next cage, too," the clerk insisted.

"And just why is that?" the man asked, beginning to show some irritation.

"Because," the clerk explained, "the one in the next cage does all the arrangements."

Show Biz

To love animals, you have to be willing to take care of them. But I quickly learned that caring for animals has its messy points. As a former clown—in fact, as the first Ronald McDonald and also Bozo—I have a real respect and empathy for those who train and care for circus animals. Their dedication sometimes goes far beyond the call of duty.

Once when I was playing Bozo the Clown, I was hired to serve as "emcee" or master of ceremonies for a children's party. The main attraction at the party—besides Bozo, of course—was a chimpanzee named Charlie who was trained to roller skate. After I introduced Charlie, he proceeded to skate around the room in a big circle, and all the children loved it. But every time he passed me, he gave me a long, strange look. I can't say I blame him. I had on my usual billowy blue-gray suit with a big white collar, a fire-engine red wig, and giant red shoes.

The third time Charlie skated past me, he just couldn't handle it anymore. He leaped across the room at me, bit my arm and tore the clown suit to shreds; and he even tried to pull off my wig! The trainer and his assistant rushed to pull us apart, and I was more shaken than hurt. Wild animals are just so unpredictable. Who would have guessed the chimp would have wanted my Bozo wig *that* much!

More recently, when a circus came to town, the public relations people for the circus invited all the local television and radio personalities to the circus parade on the way to the fair grounds. Well, somehow, they convinced *me* to ride atop one of the elephants. It wasn't the most comfortable ride, you can be sure. I had to grab onto a massive chain that was around the elephant's neck, and dig my knees behind the animal's ears.

That was bad enough, because each step the elephant took, I swayed precariously from one side to the other. But when a child spilled some popcorn on the street, well, the elephant just thought that was the greatest thing he'd ever seen. This huge beast lurched for the popcorn like a kid in a candy store, and I flew right over the top of his head. I just shut my eyes and held on to the chain for dear life, and I found myself hanging upside down over this great animal's head. I may not be able to tell you what I *will* do in the future, but you can be sure of what I *won't* do: I'll never ride another elephant!

Another time, I was talking with one guy who worked at a circus, and he told me that he gave enemas to the elephants.

"You know," he said, "you put a stepladder on the elephant's tush, and you climb up with a hose. You stick the hose in the elephant's tail and pump it full of water. Then you jump off the ladder as fast as you can."

"Doesn't the elephant ever have an accident on you?" I asked.

"Oh, sure. It happens all the time."

"But that's a stupid job. Why don't you get another?" I persisted.

"What? And give up show biz?"

Hound Dog

Hound dog stories are among the favorites from local farmers I heard around our hearthside. I guess that's because—with my three dogs—I can relate to them so well. My neighbor had an old hound who used to go with him everywhere. The dog was particularly skilled at hunting bear.

You see, the dog would bark and chase the bear up a tree, and my friend would just come along and shake the limb of the tree until the bear fell down. That's when the dog put his main skill to work. You see, my friend had trained his hound to chomp down on a male bear's most sensitive area. Then, while the bear was paralyzed with pain, the hunter would simply wrap the bear in a net, and never even have to use his gun.

This neighbor of mine was so proud of how he'd trained the dog to hunt that he just had to show a visiting relative the new method. Sure enough, the hound dog was soon hot on the trail of a bear, and within a few minutes he trapped one in a tree.

"Now hold the gun and watch this," my neighbor said. With that, he reached for the limb but slipped, falling to the ground. On cue, the hound lurched toward his master, ready to zero in on anything that fell nearby.

"To hell with the bear!" he yelled. "Shoot the dog!"

Animal Magnetism

Careful observation of animal behavior can teach you more than an entire library. For example, there's the Texas tale that distinguishes the pitfalls of youthful recklessness from the greater benefits of measured action and wise planning.

A young bull and an old bull were walking along one day, when they saw a field filled with beautiful, healthy young cows. The young bull turned to the other and said, "Let's run down there and make love to one of those cows."

"I've got a better idea," the older bull said. "Let's *walk* down there and make love to *all* of them."

Special Popcorn Turkey Dressing

This may not be one of Grandma Scott's recipes, but I'd still love to try it out at a good party.

> 6 eggs, well beaten
> 1 tsp. each, salt and pepper
> 1 sweet pepper, sliced
> 3 large onions, minced
> ½ cup red port cooking wine
> 1 cup unpopped popcorn
> 1 tsp. sugar
> Sage, to taste
> 1 large cake browned corn bread

Mix all of the ingredients and stir well. Add a small amount of water to ensure proper moisture. Stuff entire mixture into the turkey cavity, and put into 350-degree preheated oven. Bake for two hours, or until popcorn blows the turkey's rear end across the room.

V

DOWN HOME

've always thought that one of our greatest assets as Americans is our ability to laugh together. There are clearly some common threads in our sense of humor. Americans feel free to poke fun at ourselves and are free politically to laugh at and with those people in positions of authority. There's a certain accepted irreverance about ourselves and our chosen leaders that just seems to be in our blood.

Of course, people in every society get their jollies at the expense of their celebrities or officials, but nowhere is it as open as it is in the "good ole U.S.A." I once heard that there was an international medical convention in New York, and Russian doctors there discussed surgical techniques with their American colleagues.

"You know," said one Russian doctor, "we have been having great difficulties with tonsillectomies."

The American doctors were astounded. "But we've been doing them for decades," they said. "They're among our most common and successful operations!"

"Yes," said the Russian, "but you know in our country, we're not allowed to open our mouths for anything. So we have to operate from the other end!"

When I visit local rotary clubs and Jaycees groups around the country, I can always count on the common, free American sense of humor to get me on the right track with any crowd. For example, here's one approach I use to get off to a good start with any crowd: After an overly-long or overly-gracious—and some-times boring—introduction by a group's "leader," I like to turn to him or her and express my appreciation by saying, "I want to thank you for *not* giving me a tough act to follow."

Regardless of where I am, poking fun at the "big guys" this way is always sure to get a laugh. In fact, wherever I go, people love to laugh at pretty much the same jokes, no matter what ethnic or national group is the subject. There's obviously a grass-roots *American* sense of humor that permeates every nook and cranny of our varied nation.

Of course, sometimes *I'm* the one who is the butt of this common funny bone.

I get lots of letters from people who are nice enough to tell me the good ways that I've affected their lives. But then there are also those people who are somewhat less appreciative. One letter I got recently said, "Dear Mr. Scott: I hope you enjoyed your vacation, because *we* certainly did."

That must have been from an ex-girlfriend.

Sometimes when I'm home I'll just go to the nearby super-market to do some shopping, and often people will recognize me and say something nice. But other times I'll run into a person with a bone to pick, and I'll become the ready target. I was pushing my shopping cart past a fresh vegetable counter at a nearby Virginia supermarket, when I brushed past a woman who was blocking most of the aisle. When I touched her to say excuse me, she recoiled in horror. "Don't you touch me. I think you and your show stink!"

There's nothing like returning home to bring you back down to earth.

"X" Marks the Spot

Some regions have a unique sense of humor, and some towns and states have a heady competitiveness that results in some classic put-down jokes. I heard this story during a swing through the Great Lakes region.

Two Michigan fishermen were out on a lake one day, and they weren't catching a thing. They went from one spot to another, but nothing was biting.

Finally, after moving for the fifth time, they threw in their lines and the fish struck. One after the other, the fishermen pulled them into the boat.

"This place is great!" said one. "We better mark it so we can find it again tomorrow."

With that, the other drew out his pocket knife, reached over the side of the boat, and slashed an "X" on the boat right near the waterline.

"Not like that, stupid," the first one said, "What if we don't get the same boat tomorrow?"

Texas Talk

I've noticed Texans have become more temperate in their boasting in recent years, and some have even reached the point where they can laugh at themselves. For example, one dyed-in-the-wool Dallasite passed along this nugget to me:

Ireland is a small country, and very often Irish farms seem to be scaled down to fit the size of the country.

A Texan who was touring Ireland got into a conversation with an Irish farmer. "How big is your farm?" he asked.

"Well, now," said the farmer, hitching up his trousers, "You go down to that big tree there, along the stone fence to the brow of the hill, come down by way of that spotty cow standing there, turn right, then come back here to me cottage. And that's me farm."

The Texan swelled himself up with pride, and said boastfully: "Why, back home, I can get in my car and drive all day and by sundown I'll still have miles to go to reach the end of my property."

The Irishman nodded thoughtfully, then replied, "Yes, we had a car like that once, but we sold it."

Royal Flush

Some people may not go for Texas-style tall tales, but others *will* go for it—hook, line, and sinker. I heard this story recently in a Houston bar:

A traveler had wandered into that same tavern the day before and was astonished by what he saw. The bar extended as far as the eye could see, with dozens of stools for the patrons.

76

The visitor pulled up to the bar and signaled the bartender. "This is really incredible! I've heard those stories about everything being big in Texas, but until today, I never believed them."

"They're all true," said the bartender. "In fact, if I want to talk to the other bartender, way, way down at the other end of the bar, I have to call him on this phone over here."

The visitor shook his head in amazement. "Well, I guess I'll start with a draft beer."

In a moment, the bartender returned with an enormous glass of beer that would have been a large pitcher anywhere else. "That'll be eight dollars," said the bartender.

"Whew," the visitor said, pulling out his wallet.

A little while later, the visitor was finishing his beer, and asked directions to the washroom so he could relieve himself.

"You see that hall at the end of the bar?" the bartender said. "Just go down there and make a right."

The visitor squinted into the distance, shook his head, and made his way unsteadily into the hallway. Once there, however, he lost his bearings, and instead of making a right, he made a left out the exit. His head unclear from his large drink, he stumbled across the alleyway into the open door of a health club, and instead of a toilet, he found himself facing a large but deserted indoor pool.

"Wow. Everything but everything is bigger in Texas."

His drink getting the better of him, however, he lost his balance once again and slipped into the pool. When he came sputtering up to the surface, he caught sight of the lifeguard and cried: "Don't flush, don't flush!"

Southern Belles

People in the South seem to go about life in a different way than the frenetic Yankees or the people out West. A Southern woman, for instance, has every bit of the determination and strength of her sisters in the rest of the country, but without the hard edge. Below the Mason-Dixon Line, women are tough—they just don't appear that way when you first meet them.

For example, when a Southern woman is told something that she knows is an exaggeration or overstatement, she may reply, "Well, I declare" or "Charmin'." It took me a while to discover that "I declare" is the Southern equivalent of "Bull - - - -!"

Man of Conviction

A good friend and former neighbor of mine told me another story that reflects the ultimate in Southern gentility.

A Georgia man convicted of murder stood in the courtroom, with head bowed, listening while the judge passed sentence on him.

"You will be taken to the state prison," the judge intoned solemnly, "and thirty days hence, you will be executed by having a charge of electricity passed through your body. And may God have mercy on your soul. Do you have anything to say to this court?"

The unhappy prisoner said he did. "First, I'd like to thank my lawyer," he began. "I know he was court appointed, and didn't want to take the case. But he did the best he could, anyway."

He turned to the prosecutor, and said, "And I don't bear you any malice, sir. I know you were just carrying out the law.

78

"And I'd like to say to the jury," he went on. "You paid attention and rendered a verdict you thought was right. I know you didn't have anything against me personally, nor do I bear any of you a grudge.

"But Judge." He paused and looked at the bench. "You just tore it with me."

Train Porter

Washington D.C. may resemble a fast-paced Northern city nowadays, but believe me, it's a *Southern* city all the way. Right down to the White House, the architecture is patterned after the classic ante-bellum styles that can be seen throughout the South. There have always been grand parties and important affairs in Washington, but it's only been in the last ten or twenty years that the city has seen a more metropolitan nightlife like that of the northeast's bigger cities. But no matter what, Washington will always call the South its home.

When I was working there, the laid-back attitude of the D.C. Southerners around me used to help to put things in perspective. For example, I was in Union Station one day, and the way it was arranged, the Northern trains came in on one level, and the Southern trains on the lower tracks. Well, one day, a train porter told me he was on the lower tracks when there was a terrible accident.

"I was waiting on the Southern tracks," he said, "when I heard the eight o'clock coming in from New York. I heard the brakes squeal and I heard this tremendous crash. I looked up and I saw the concrete start to break. The next thing I saw, the Northern train was sitting down there on the Southern track. I said to myself, 'That ain't right.' "

79

Barkeep's Bane

In contrast to this slower, Southern pace of life, many people from the big cities in the East have a reputation for being extremely demanding and impatient. Sometimes it doesn't sit too well with small-town folks. A tavern owner told me about a Northerner who recently walked into his bar and ordered a drink.

"I want a very dry martini," he said to the bartender. "Five parts gin to one part vermouth. As a matter of fact, you can make it six parts gin, and then walk past it carrying a bottle of vermouth."

"Coming right up," said the bartender. "Shall I add a lemon twist?"

"Look," said the man. "If I'd wanted lemonade, I'd have ordered lemonade."

Border Bandit

On a tour through the Southwest, I saw firsthand the problems they're having dealing with smuggling of contraband over the border. They're using new methods to catch the outlaws, but a local businessman told me that some of the smugglers are getting awfully clever.

It seems that several times a week, a man on a bicycle with a basket of sand attached to it would ride up to the customs station at the United States–Mexico border. He never had anything to declare, and though the customs inspectors plowed diligently through the basket of sand, they always came away empty handed.

This ritual went on, week in, week out, but the agents never found anything. Finally, their curiosity got the best of them, and the next time the man rode up, the chief inspector said to him, "Three or four times a week, you ride up here, on a bicycle with a basket of sand. We know you're smuggling something, but we can't figure out what it is. Tell us, just to satisfy our curiosity. We promise not to press charges. What are you smuggling?"

"Bicycles," the man answered.

Sautéed Seagull

When you talk about the coast of Maine, the first thing that often comes to mind is lobsters. But in my trips to the coastal areas, what I remember most of all are the seagulls.

Once, while vacationing in Maine, I was especially amazed at the seagulls that were always around in large numbers. "Aren't they good for anything?" I asked a native one morning.

"Not so far as I know," the native replied.

"Why don't you catch 'em and eat 'em?" I inquired.

"Well, I'll tell you," said the native. "If you put a seagull and a brick in the oven at the same time, the brick would get done first. And it would taste better."

Yankee Humor

One thing I notice when I visit rural areas of the Northeast is that there's a certain amount of pride in one-upmanship among the local residents.

A favorite local story that I've heard around in New England involves a farmer who wanted to retire, but had been unable to sell his small farm by the lake.* When winter came and snow covered the ground, a city slicker came by and saw the vast expanse of white snow. He offered the farmer what he considered to be a ridiculously low price for the property, and to his surprise, the farmer accepted the offer. The city man was gleeful at his bargain.

It wasn't until springtime that he found out that most of the "land" that he had bought was really a snow-covered pond.

Crazy Sue

The greatest misconception there is about Yankee humor is the belief that there's no such thing. It's there, all right, with a slap so dry it'll make your mouth pucker. Though some New England towns are so small the residents have to take turns being the town drunk, in every one of them there are a few people who are referred to as "eccentrics." Crazy Sue was one such person, and a lot of people in the Berkshire community where she lived have stories to tell about her.

One time, I've heard, Crazy Sue was fishing in a stream when a well-known local lawyer and his doctor friend caught sight of her.

"Now Crazy Sue, there's no fish in that little stream," they said. "What can you possibly hope to catch?"

"The devil," Sue snapped, not missing a beat.

---

* Similar accounts of this and the next two stories may be found in "Summerscope: A Guide To The Berkshires," the summer magazine of *The Transcript*, North Adams, Mass., August 5, 1983.

"And what, may we ask, are you using for bait?" they laughed.

"Why, doctors and lawyers, of course."

Crazy Sue was always being teased by the local children, but she always got the better of them—particularly on her favorite subject, religion. One time, a group of youths stopped her on the street and proceeded to tease her as usual.

"Sue, Sue! Did you hear the devil died?"

"Oh, when?" Sue replied.

"Day before yesterday," the youths snickered.

"Oh, you poor, fatherless children," Sue sniffed.

Reprieve Replay

Friends of mine from Great Barrington, Massachusetts, tell me that when a local farmer's wife died a few years ago, it caused more than just a little stir. From what they tell me, the hearse carrying the body hit the cemetery's stone gatepost. The coffin flew from the back of the hearse, broke open on the ground, and revived the "dead" woman. She not only revived, but she lived another five years before passing away!

Again, the funeral procession meandered through the town. As the hearse approached the cemetery, the farmer leaned toward the driver. "Be careful, now. Don't hit that post again."

Back Side and Bay Side

A visitor from another region isn't always familiar with local slang and expressions that the residents take for granted. In the Cape Cod shore area, the term "bay side" refers to areas of a given property closest to the bay, and "back side" refers to areas away from the bay.

.One time, a Washington neighbor of mine vacationing in Cape Cod admitted to being a little shocked at the words that came out of his otherwise prim landlady's mouth. All he wanted to know was the best place to catch some sun, he said. She looked him straight in the eye and said, "The best place is on the Back Side."

If that wasn't enough, my neighbor said, he couldn't get used to the waitress's brusque manner in a local bistro.

"This steak is tough," my friend complained to the waitress.

"It's tougher when there's none," she said.

Local Yankee Expressions

As I said earlier, I love regional dialects and expressions. For example, I'm a great coffee fan, but Northeasterners have me beat by a mile, especially in the way they extol the brew. Yankees are said to be such lovers of coffee that if you "put a bag of coffee in the mouth of hell, a Yankee will be sure to go after it."

Here are a few gems from the country's birthplace:

- An early riser is said to "pry up the sun with a crowbar."

- When a hired hand goofs off, he's "looking for salt

pork and sundown." Down South, it's "6 o'clock and payday."

- "Slower than a hoptoad in hot tar."
- "Faster than a cat lapping chain lightning."
- "Safe as in God's pocket."

Here are some more favorites of mine from the Northeast that deal with a subject close to my heart: the weather.

- "We have two seasons: winter and the Fourth of July."
- "New England climate consists of nine months winter and three months late in the fall."
- "Fogs so thick you could cut 'em up into chunks with your jackknife."
- "Fog's so durn thick this mornin' you kin hardly spit." *Out west,* they say "It's so dry you have to prime yourself to spit."
- "It wuz cold enough to freeze two dry rags together."—or "Colder than a welldigger's kneecap."
- "Wind blew so hard it blew straight up and down."—Or, "So windy, a chicken laid the same egg three times."

Deficit Spending

I've learned that you don't underestimate a Yankee's ability to put the most technical discussions on a down-to-earth level. A friend of mine was discussing the economy and deficit spending with an acquaintance in a Cape Cod tavern one day, when he was treated to a bit of down-home wisdom.

"No sir," said the Cape Codder, "I don't hold with all these new ideas. I've allus made it a point to never wash more'n I can hang out."

Epitaphs

Of all the written histories of our nation and its people, few are as telling as the words that are etched on tombstones in the countryside. On tombstones we can see the stories of people as they really were, how they wanted to be remembered, or how their neighbors remembered them.

One of my favorites was quoted by President Harry Truman, who, in reminiscing about his own 1948 election, recalled a tombstone he saw out in Boot Hill. It was very simple, and to the point, just like Harry himself:

Here lies Jack Davis
He done his damdest

Here are just a few more selected ones* that I love:

From Georgia peanut country:

Here lies Bill
Extremely still
Died from a chill

On Jonathan Fiddle:

On the 22nd of June
Jonathan Fiddle
Went Out of Tune

---

* Several can also be found in Henry R. Morton, *Comic Epitaphs* (Mt. Vernon, New York: The Peter Pauper Press, 1957).

Down Home

Here lies an honest man—here lies a politician—
there must be two fellas in that hole

On the same subject, here's one on John Strange, the
lawyer:

> Here Lies An
> Honest Lawyer

> That Is Strange

Legend on hypochondriac's tombstone:

> I told you I was sick

On an author:

> He has written finis

On a painter:

> A finished artist

On a fisherman:

> He's hooked it

On a coal miner:

> Gone underground for good

On a photographer:

> Taken from life

On a gardener:

> Transplanted

Miscellaneous Epitaphs

Here lies Pecos Bill
He always lied
And always will:
He once lied loud
He now lies still

———

When from the tomb
To meet his doom
He rises amidst sinners:
Take him to dwell
In Heaven or Hell
Whichever serves
Big dinners

———

Here lies
Hermina Kuntz
To virtue unknown:
Jesus, rejoice!
At last
She sleeps alone

———

Sacred to the remains of
Jonathan Thompson
A Pious Christian and
Affectionate Husband
His disconsolate widow
Continues to carry on
His grocery business
At the old stand on
Main Street: Cheapest
And best prices in town

———

Down Home

Death's advantage
Over life I spye:
Here one husband with
Two wyves may lye

———

Poker Jim Wilkins
His last full house

———

Mary Weary, housewife
Dere friends I am going
Where washing ain't done
Or cooking or sewing:
Don't mourn for me now
Or weep for me never:
For I go to do nothing
For ever and ever!

———

Beneath these stones
Do lie
Back to back
My wife and I:
When the last loud trump
Shall blow,
If she gets up
I'll just lie low

VI

ALL WORK ... ◆ ◆ ◆

here are at least three ingredients for a happy life: first, to have good health; second, to have a family that you love and that loves you; and third, to have a decent job that you're happy with.

I think a job is awfully important—but not because of any prestigious title, responsibility, or power that may come with it. No—the primary contribution of a good job is to enhance your pride and self-esteem.

Considering the fact that people spend more waking hours on the job than they do at home, you can't deny the impact your job can have on your life. A job can't be expected to be rewarding in every way, of course, but the happiest people I've seen are those who enjoy what they do and do what they enjoy.

Of course, you don't usually move right into that ultimate

job that's going to provide you with supreme happiness. When I first started out at NBC, I was the lowest man on the totem pole—a page. But my position really didn't matter at all to me. I was perfectly happy to start at the bottom if it meant I had a chance to rise in an organization I admired. My main job at one time was fetching hot dogs for the other NBC staffers. Yet, I don't think anybody ever looked down at me in that job, and if they did, I really don't care. Most people knew that being a lowly page was the way you got started in the business, and I was willing to do anything to be in my chosen field.

I was so proud that I had finally gotten to work at NBC, that I sent my first dollar that I ever earned there to then-chairman of NBC General David Sarnoff, and I asked him to sign it. When he returned it, I also got Arthur Godfrey to sign it. It has hung on my wall ever since. Years later, when I told the general this story, he asked, "Where is the dollar now?"

"It's still on the wall in my rec room," I said.

He replied, "You're losing interest!"

Because my job allows me to be upbeat and spontaneous, I get a lot of mail from people who tell me funny things about their jobs. I really think people appreciate that you can take your sense of humor with you to work. A light touch now and then can help to lighten the load for everyone.

Sometimes, I admit, people misunderstand when I poke fun. In fact, people have written to me, "Willard, you should be ashamed of yourself—you're anti-management!" Well I'm not anti-management. I love NBC, and I've been with them for a long time. But I'll never pass up an opportunity to give the management team—and particularly our crack NBC vice-presidents—a little friendly ribbing now and then.

One of the things that I love to ride management about— and I'm sure this is true of almost any company—is their super-cautious need for high-priced *outside* advice. Forget the fact that we're on the set, day in and day out. When something's not clicking in the ratings, management's always on the horn to the "experts," the consultants.

All Work . . .

Even back in my radio days, when some deejays were involved in the "payola" scandal for accepting gratuities to promote certain artists, our station's management team decided to hire outside experts. Their mission: to find out if *we* had accepted any favors from the artists we broadcast. They spent countless thousands of dollars to have this team of stern-looking men ask us questions about our relationships with the artists and the record distributors that we aired.

Now, that may sound fair enough at first glance. But it wouldn't have taken a genius to figure out that management really had nothing to worry about. You see, ours was a. Big Bands-sound format, and practically every artist we played had either died or retired a long time past. Even record distributors had little to gain from our station. After all, they certainly couldn't expect any upsurge in record sales, especially from a program that catered to nostalgia. Besides, most of the recordings we played were hard to come by.

Nonetheless, I broke down and confessed.

"Yes, yes," I blurted out under this third degree. "One time I accepted a deck of playing cards from a major record company, and, yes, I *had* played their Montovani records on the air!"

Ah, confession is good for the soul.

Silly enough as this may seem, you still might give our execs high marks for being thorough. Unfortunately, as with other big corporations, when it comes to overlooking the obvious, television management really goes overboard. As the great radio personality Fred Allen used to say, the definition of an NBC vice-president is a man who comes into his office each morning at 9:00 to find a molehill on his desk, and then spends the remaining eight hours trying to make a mountain out of it.

In television, not a step is made without expert advice from top-dollar consultants—the more expensive the better. But hardly a question is posed to the people on the air. You see, if there's a slackening in the spring ratings, management gets apoplectic and runs for "corrective" advice. They'll do anything to give birth to a bright, profitable new idea. Someone told me that you can always tell when it's spring at the RCA building—that's when the NBC vice-presidents crawl up the carpets to spawn— thanks again Fred.

Before you know what's happening, they tinker around with the set, change the show's format ever so slightly, and hold their breaths for a few months until the next ratings sweep. Pretty soon, they've spent half a million dollars to answer the question: "What's going wrong?" Whatever the advice, it rarely helps the ratings anyway. But it does get management off our backs for a few months.

Management's insistence on finding out what's wrong isn't the funniest part of the whole situation. What gets me is that even if the ratings are doing wonderfully, management gets itchy. They run to the consultants to find out what they're doing right! I don't know about you, but where I come from, people say, "If it ain't broke, don't fix it."

But that's not true at NBC. I once told Bryant Gumbel that NBC had missed a sure bet one recent Christmas, with all the furor over the Cabbage Patch dolls. They should have come out with NBC vice-president dolls—you wind them up and they write memos.

While I think NBC's management team is top notch, I don't put too much stock in "professional" critics like outside consul- tants. Sometimes, the things they hate the most are the most popular with the people. For instance, not too long ago I ap- peared on the show dressed as Carmen Miranda. If you saw me, you know I'm not just talking bananas on the head. No sir, I went the whole shebang. I put on a dress, wore earrings, platform shoes, a fruit-filled headdress—like everything else I do in life, I went 100 percent, all the way.

I really wasn't sure if I could pull it off. But one day as I was working with my Rototiller in my garden, I came up with some great lyrics, and I felt I just had to try it. After all, that's what enjoying life is all about—being spontaneous, and having the courage of your convictions. Like most other fun and good things in life, a risk was involved. Fortunately, that's what my job is all about, too. I knew it was going to be either a hit, or a big bomb. One way or the other, I knew we would make a huge impression.

Predictably, the critics hated it. But the people loved it! In fact, it became a sensation. Wherever I went, traveling for "Today," people screamed, "Do Carmen! Do Carmen!" It just confirmed for me that—regardless of what the critics and outside consultants say—as long as you please the people, you're going to be a hit.

But there was one incident in particular that really showed me where I could find the best advice in the world. During a particularly low-rating period of the "Today" show, the management hired a high-powered consulting firm to jazz things up. It must have cost them at least $250,000 just to sign a contract with these guys. And they did the usual—a new set was constructed, costing another quarter million. So by then, NBC's ante had been raised to a neat half-million dollars.

I was flying across the country on one of my many trips for the "Today" show, and had a nice coach seat next to a lovely grandmotherly-type woman. We exchanged polite—but infrequent—conversation for the first thousand miles of the trip. But after granny knocked back her third martini, things began to change.

"You know," she said, "I used to watch your show, but I just can't anymore. They rush you through the weather, and never give it enough time. Half of the subjects they feature are dull and of no interest at all. Then, when they finally *do* get a good interview, they always cut it off too short."

Just my luck. A thousand miles to go and I'm stuck next to a lady who thinks she's David Hartman's mother. I couldn't find a parachute, so I just settled in for a long flight.

"Just who decides the content of the show?" she continued, biting out the pimiento from her olive. "It's all so shallow. Everything is so frantic. The hosts talk too fast, and they never seem to listen when the people they interview try to answer. They always cut them off—'no more time!' That's what's wrong with your show, sonny."

Well, I had to admire her spunk, even if I may not have liked what I was hearing. But when I got back on the set of "Today," I was in for a surprise. They had just gotten the latest consultants' report. Wouldn't you know, it was, point for point, exactly what granny had told me on the jet! She had given me for free the same advice that had cost NBC a half-million dollars.

You can come up with your own moral to that story: Perhaps something like, "Big corporations should listen more to little old ladies." Or maybe, "Little old ladies should go to work for consulting firms." As for me, I wouldn't like that. If they all worked for consultants, then I never would have had the pleasure of meeting such a grand dame on one of my trips. After all, if she had been a consultant, she would have been riding in first class—not coach, as I was.

Letter Perfect

People *do* love to put in their two cents, and I have files full of letters to prove it. But one letter I received stood out because of what it didn't say. You see, we always start the show in the morning with a round of "hellos" and "good mornings." Well this letter writer had this to say about that: "Good morning, Tom; good morning, Jane; good morning, Gene; good morning, Willard. Goodbye 'Today,' 'Good Morning, America.' "

My favorite letter of all time, I received in my radio days. "Dear Mr. Scott, I think you are the best disk jockey in Washington. I think you play the best music and you have the nicest voice of anybody on the air. Please excuse the crayon; they won't let us have anything sharp in here."

Insurance Foibles

Companies also receive a large number of letters from people asking for information or just saying what's on their minds. Here are some samples of letters written to life and health insurance companies that are nothing short of surprising:

- "I cannot get sick pay. I have six children. Can you tell me why?"

- "I am forwarding my marriage certificate with my three children—one of which was a mistake as you will see."

- "You have changed my little boy to a little girl. Will this make a difference?"

- "Unless I get my husband's money very soon, I will be forced to lead an immoral life."

- "This is my eighth child. What are you going to do about it?"

- "In accordance with instructions, I have given birth to twins in the enclosed envelope."

- "I want money as quick as I can get it. I have been in bed with the doctor for two weeks and it hasn't done me any good. If things don't improve, I'll have to get another one."

- "I have no children as yet as my husband is a bus driver and works night and day."

- "I am writing to say my baby is more than two years old. When do I get my money?"

- "I'm glad to report that my husband, who was reported missing, is dead."

- "In answer to your letter, I have given birth to a boy weighing ten pounds. I hope this is satisfactory."

- "Please find for certain, is my husband dead? The man I live with can't eat nothin' till he knows."

- "Mrs. Jones has not had clothing for a year and has been visited regularly by the clergy."

Face the Nation

Sometimes, back when I was on radio, people used to call in to the station and actually talk directly to us. When they did, and we were able to meet our audience "face to face," as it were. It was a real eye-opener to find out who we appealed to.

One time, during a snowstorm, we were deluged with calls from our listeners who were concerned about schools being open and whether or not certain functions would take place as planned. They would say something like, "I wanna know if John Marshall High School is going to be closed today." It was a valuable public service, of course, and we were glad to provide the information as best we knew.

During this flood of calls in the middle of a blizzard, one guy phoned who was obviously inebriated. "Could ya, could ya, could ya pleeeaase tell me, will the liquor stores be open today?"

Who Works?

I guess in my line of work, I have to expect to come across some strange types now and then. Some people have even suggested that I attract weird people, because of the way I do my job. In any case, I do love my work, and I really can't understand people who don't like to put in an honest day on the job. But apparently there are quite a few folks out there who will go to great lengths to avoid any labor.

Senator Orrin Hatch of Utah once confided to me that the number of people in the American work force has been grossly overestimated. Here are some statistics that he gave me to back up his claim.

"The population of this country is about 215 million, but there are 92 million over 60 years of age, leaving 123 million to do the work. People under 21 total 103 million, leaving 20 million to do the work. Then there are 4 million people employed by the federal government, and that leaves 16 million to do the work. Three million are in the Armed Services, leaving 13 million to do the work. Deduct 12,800,000—the number in state and city offices, and that leaves 200,000 to do the work.

"There are 126,000 in hospitals, and so forth, and that leaves 74,000 to do the work. But 62,000 of these are bums or others who won't work, so that leaves 12,000 to do the work. Now it may interest you to know that there are 11,998 people in jail, so that leaves just two people to do the work . . . AND THAT'S YOU AND ME, BROTHER, AND I'M TIRED OF DOING EVERYTHING BY MYSELF!"

Job Interview

I've always thought that job hunters had an awfully rough time. But Senator John East of North Carolina says that employers may have it even tougher—especially when they are trying to evaluate the worth of an out-of-work politician. Here's a favorite story he told me about one boss's plight.

An employer was interviewing for a vacancy within his business. He interviewed three men: a mathematician, a statistician, and a politician. He asked each man the same question, "What is two plus two?," and he got the following responses:

The mathematician said, without a moment of hesitation, "That is very simple. Two plus two is four."

The statistician pondered for a moment and then explained, "The sum of two plus two lies somewhere between three and five, with a 100 percent probability that the answer will be four."

The politician looked at the employer for a moment, paused, and with the greatest sincerity said, "What do you want it to be?"

Voice of Experience

There's nothing like offering an untried young person the chance to earn a living. But there's also something to be said for making "experience only" a requirement of some jobs. My uncle used to tell a tale to illustrate that sometimes you don't find this out until it's too late.

The driver of a soft-drink truck hired a teenage boy to help him load and unload cases of drinks. The boy spoke with a slight stutter, but that was no drawback as he was an able and willing worker.

They had delivered several cases of drinks to a little country store one day, and were driving back to the main highway. At the intersection, the driver stopped to look for oncoming traffic "Do you see anything coming over there?" he asked his young helper.

"No-no sir—" the boy replied haltingly, whereupon the driver pulled onto the main road, and the boy finished his observation, "—No-nothing but a bi-big red truck!"

Kid-Gloved Linemen

I can be free and spontaneous when I'm on the "Today" show, but I still have to watch what I say. People may think some public figures are a bit too free with their words, and they go beyond the limit of acceptability. Sometimes, though, there's good reason for strong words. One telephone worker told me that the supervisor of a group of phone company workers called in two of his linemen for a reprimand. "Men," he said, "a lady called me today to complain about the language she says she heard you use. She says it was some of the strongest profanity she ever heard. What did you say, anyway?"

One of the men explained. "Aw, it wasn't anything, chief," he said. "Fred was working up above me on the pole, and all I said was, 'Fred, please don't drop no more of that hot lead down my neck.' "

Road Workers

Certain jobs have a reputation for involving hard, back-breaking labor. But whenever I see road workers while I'm driving along the highway, I always remember a road crew foreman who used to live near my farm. His workers, it seems, weren't so diligent.

This foreman had a bull gang of about a half dozen or so men who were driven out every morning to do repair work on county roads. One morning, after arriving at the job site, the foreman discovered that they had forgotten to bring along the shovels.

"All right," he said. "I'll take the truck and go back and get them. You guys will just have to lean on each other until I get back."

Delivery Blues

In my youth, I used to earn spending money by delivering packages for a local store. I think that's when I first learned not to use ten-dollar words for ten-cent business.

"I think this is your package, sir," I said to a man who had answered his door. "It's the right address, but the name is obliterated."

"No, it's not mine, then," the man answered. "My name is Franklin."

Ask a Silly Question

A friend of mine who worked in the credit department of a big department store informed me that I hadn't cornered the market on strange customers.

A woman was opening a charge account and was being questioned by my friend, the clerk. "What is your occupation?" the clerk asked.

"I'm a licensed practical nurse," the woman answered.

"And what is your husband's occupation?"

"He's a manufacturer."

"Children?"

"No, he manufactures aluminum siding."

All in a Day's Work

The owner of a business near me in New York was known for being a hard taskmaster. One day, he was walking through his warehouse and he saw a teenage boy sitting on a box, reading a comic book.

"How much are you paid a week?" he asked the boy.

"A hundred twenty-five dollars," the boy answered.

The owner pulled out his wallet, extracted that amount from it, and handed it to the boy. "Here's a week's wages," he said angrily. "Now, get out of here!"

Then the man turned to his warehouse superintendent. "Where did you hire that deadbeat?" he asked?

"I didn't," said the superintendent. "He just delivered a package and was waiting for his receipt."

The Hard Way

When I was growing up, one of the liveliest spots in town was a local diner that was the hangout for the teenagers. The diner's owner had a reputation for hiring people with no experience whatsoever, because he didn't like to have to pay them anything. Sometimes, he wound up with less on his hands than he bargained for.

The owner of the restaurant once hired a waitress whose "elevator didn't go to the top." "Why haven't you finished refilling those salt shakers like I told you to?" he asked her.

"Because," she replied, "it's hard to push the salt through those little holes."

Coffee Break

With the rowdy kids at this diner, it didn't take long for even the dullest of the workers to catch on to the art of the snappy comeback. But sometimes they were just too sensitive.

A man sat down at the counter in the restaurant and ordered coffee. "Looks a little like rain, doesn't it?" he said to the waitress as he stirred sugar into his cup.

"Yes, it does," she replied. "But it's coffee, just the same."

VII

OUT OF THE MOUTHS OF BABES . . .

hough I'm often seen as the gregarious, outgoing type, my family has always been at the center of my life. I never had a brother or sister, you see, so perhaps, being an only child, I go overboard in emphasizing the value of a diverse family.

Children in particular are an inspiration to me. I have two children of my own, and I do whatever I can to be around them as much as possible. Kids have that marvelous sense of wonder and an unrestrained honesty and enthusiasm so often lost in the adult world.

Sometimes I still catch a glimmer of this unique joie de vivre in adults when I travel. Speaking to veterans' groups or the local Moose Lodge gives me a rare opportunity to see grown men let their hair down, dress up in strange hats and clothes, and play practical jokes on each other. It's great fun!

In part I think it's because I've retained my childlike outlook that my relationship with my children has become closer and more forthright. Sometimes I feel sorry when I hear a teenager on the phone with his parents; it sounds more like he's talking with his lawyer than with good old Mom or Dad. In our household, we don't have any such "business conferences." My girls, Mary and Sally, feel free to talk with me about practically anything with a degree of openness that seems to be exceptional nowadays.

Outside my family, kids mean almost as much to me as they do inside. On a more personal level, I've taught Bible school for children; on the professional level, I've made appearances with the Muppets. Frankly, I owe my career to the many shows and performances I've done for kids—in any number of roles, from Bozo the Clown to Ronald McDonald to Commander Retro. Kids can really be interesting people, if we only take the time to listen to them.

I count myself especially lucky that I just seem to have a good rapport with kids—possibly because we have a similar approach to the little joys of life. I love their infectious enthusiasm, their openness, and their sense of excitement. Our younger years are also our most honest. It's only after we reach a certain age that we seem to pass that time of innocence. I would say that by the time a child gets to be around six to eight years old, he or she starts to abandon this childlike openness. Until then, however, children have few pretenses; they are particularly direct and up-front.

In particular, I love kids' capacity to get excited—I mean to the point where they are really gushing. Children can make a game out of anything, or make anything a cause for celebration. When the girls were younger, I used to make breakfast for them. I'd announce, as enthusiastically as possible, "Guess what! We're going to have oatmeal this morning!"

"Yea, oatmeal!" they'd scream. Picking up on my enthusiasm, they'll run around the table four times, barking like dogs or doing some other crazy, wonderful thing.

I miss that quality in adults. Older folks tend to get awfully blasé sometimes for my taste. As Peggy Lee would say "Is that all there is to that?"

There's a passage in the Bible that I like to remember, in which Jesus discusses the importance of the childlike quality that we all should maintain: "Unless you turn and become like little children, you will never see the kingdom of Heaven." And you'll enjoy everything you see en route, as well.

Yipes! Snipes!

I had a wonderful time as a child. Just mention the Boy Scouts to me and that conjures up a lot of happy memories. I loved the camaraderie of camping and scouting in the great outdoors, and the good times of learning to get along with me new friends.

As a newcomer to Scouting, I went through the traditional pranks. Because they are learning so much about the world, children find things every day that they never knew existed. So it seemed perfectly reasonable to me that we'd hunt for an animal I had never heard of.

We'd be taken on a long, circuitous hike through the woods, and we were told with all sincerity that the key to survival in the wild was to learn how to hunt for snipes. The older kids made us promise that we wouldn't come back empty-handed, and so we followed their instructions to the letter.

We'd stand in the middle of the woods, holding a sack of some sort, and stamp our feet and yell, "Here snipe, here snipe!" Then we'd wait for a while, and start yelling and stamping again.

Hours passed, but no snipes came. Only after we were truly exhausted did some begin to catch on: A snipe hunt was just a glorified wild-goose chase. Others like me refused to give up, and the older ones finally had to come get us.

Of course, most parents informed their kids later on that there really were no such things as snipes. They had just become victims of a gag that's been going on for generations. Unfortunately, my parents never told me. If you can believe it, it wasn't until recently that I found out that the wool had been pulled over old Willard's eyes for a long, long time.

Mystical Mumblings

Another time, we novices were all gathered together to learn an ancient Indian chant. By repeating the chant over and over, we were told, we would develop great insight into the greatest secrets of the world.

Standing by the campfire, we were all told to repeat the special phrase: "Oh-wah, tagoo, Siam."

Again and again we repeated this mystical chant, until finally, the more experienced boys couldn't contain themselves any longer and started laughing and "honking." We realized we'd been had, expounding to the skies, "Oh what a goose I am!"

Goofing

One time in my boyhood, my friends and I were riding in an old jeep along some dirt road in West Virginia. We were barreling down a mountain on hairpin curves, and horsing around more than we should have.

When we turned one bend in the route, the road simply stopped at the side of another large hill. Going too fast to come to a full stop, we crashed into the hill and parts of the car went flying everywhere.

An unshaven, Beech-Nut-chewing old farmer was sitting on a beat-up old upholstered sofa next to an ancient "ringer" washing machine on his front porch.

"What yew boys doing?" he asked as we pulled ourselves out of the wreck.

"Oh, we were just goofing around," I said.

He spit out some Beech-Nut, and continued to rock.

"Looks to me," he finally said, "like you ran out of goof."

Tyke Tycoon

A long time ago, when I was performing as Bozo the Clown, I was assigned to open a shopping center in Washington. As I was joking around, this little five-year-old came up to me with his mother and father.

The father was an imposing sort of guy in his mid-fifties, wearing a blue pinstripe "power" suit, horn-rimmed glasses, and sporting great, lambchop sideburns. Naturally, he was chomping on a big, fat cigar.

The mother was obviously the second or third wife, because

she was only twenty-eight or thirty, and kind of a knockout. I don't remember who it was who said, "You owe your success to your first wife, and you owe your second wife to your success."

As it turned out, the father was the builder and owner of the shopping center. His kid was a bit precocious, almost sounding like a miniature executive, and he asked all kinds of businesslike questions. Finally, apparently bent on impressing me with a verbal *coup de grace*, he looked me straight in the eye and said with a broad flourish of his hand:

"You know, Bozo, my mommy says that when my daddy dies, all this will be mine."

Bozo's Breath

One time, I was doing an appearance as Bozo at the Officers Club over near National Airport in Washington. It was Easter week, and there were kids all over the place having a great time.

After I did my bit, one of the guys said, "Well, Bozo, how about a drink."

"I really can't," I said reluctantly. "Not while I'm in this clown suit. Some kid might see me."

"Ah, come on, you're all through anyway. Just come inside."

So I went to the back of the bar, hoping no one would notice me, and had myself a couple of good swigs of my favorite whiskey.

After I was through, I went back outside and a little kid came running up to me. "Bozo, Bozo!" he yelled, squeaking my nose. "I got here late, and I thought I'd missed you."

So we shook hands and I signed an autograph for him. As he walked away, however, he called out to his mother loud enough for all the world to hear: "Mommy, Bozo smells just like daddy."

Holding a Job

Sometimes, of course, kids don't get impressed very easily. One time, a man introduced me to his five-year-old son, saying, "Willard Scott used to be Ronald McDonald."

The child didn't say anything, so the father pressed on.

"Mr. Scott also used to be Bozo the Clown."

Again, no response from the kid.

"Willard Scott also used to be on the Mickey Mouse Show."

The child slowly looked from me to his father, and said, "Mr. Scott can't hold a job—can he?"

Mistaken Identity

I have found that the literal honesty of kids may be refreshing or devastating, depending on the circumstances. So has Senator Chic Hecht of Nevada. When he was running for reelection a while ago, his wife and daughters accompanied him on the campaign trail. His daughters, aged four and six at the time, were passing out cards with the senator's name on them, and everyone made a fuss because they were Senator Hecht's daughters.

A small girl approached Senator Hecht's young daughter, Lori, and asked her name, but Lori only replied, "Senator Hecht's daughter."

Thinking that her daughter was developing a bit of an identity crisis, Mrs. Hecht became alarmed and took Lori aside.

"When someone asks you your name," she said, "you are Lori—not Senator Hecht's daughter."

111

A few minutes later, some cameramen came by and saw the cards Lori was handing out, and called out, "Hey, you're Senator Hecht's daughter!"

Lori burst into tears. "I thought I was, but my Mama just told me I'm not!"

Schooltime

For many children, the idea of going to school can be frightening. A former neighborhood boy, Andrew, was just the opposite: he was so impatient he couldn't wait to start. But as it turned out, his impatience got the best of him.

Little Andrew was quite impressed when his older brother David started to school. But he was simply awestruck when David learned to read, and he could hardly wait to start to school himself so he could master this amazing skill.

But after all the anticipation, he came home from his first day thoroughly dejected and dispirited. Indeed, he announced that he was so disgusted with public education that he wasn't going back.

His parents were puzzled by this radical change of attitude. "Why, Andrew," said his father, "for months you've been looking forward to starting school. It's all you've talked about. And now you don't want to go back. What's the matter? What happened today, anyway?"

As it turned out, it wasn't what happened; it was what didn't happen, Andrew explained. "We painted pictures and had milk and cookies and recess and everything. But I was there all day, and they didn't teach me to read!"

Talkin' Proper

Where I grew up, a lot of folks didn't have a college education. So it was a big deal when their kids started to make that giant step. Many people expect a child to return from school a changed person. The children return changed, all right, but usually not in the way the parents expected. So some folks just make the best of it.

A farmer and his wife watched with pride as their only daughter boarded a train that would take her away to begin her freshman year at the state university.

A few weeks later, she came home for the holidays. "Ma, Pa," she said as they drove away from the depot. "I've got a confession to make. I ain't a virgin anymore."

The farmer looked at his wife sorrowfully. "You hear that, Ma?" he said sadly. "We send her away to college and she still says 'ain't.' "

Language Barrier

Formal education is wonderful, of course, but nothing can replace the strong guiding hand of one's family in passing along tradition and teaching the difference between right and wrong. Still, the fast pace of these times may run far ahead of old-fashioned values. I recently overheard one elderly woman talking to her granddaughter in the park, and the oldster was clearly several steps behind the youngster. She said, "Granddaughter, there are two words I want you to promise me you'll never use. One is 'swell' and the other is 'lousy.' "

"Okay, Grandmother," the little girl answered agreeably. "What are they?"

VIII
TALES THE OLD-TIMERS TELL

Among the more incredible stories I've ever heard are those spun by the true masters of the art—the old-timers. Maybe that's because they've had the time to perfect their considerable skill. Even today, I can sit spellbound listening to these oldsters for hours on end, if for no other reason than to contemplate the images their stories bring to mind. They often reach back into their youth and recall a world in which people lived close to the land and savored the simpler things in life.

When I was a boy, my grandfather used to tell me about his adventures when he was travelling out West in a wagon with his father. I listened to one story after another through many a long night, savoring the details of the trip, imagining myself in his place, and marvelling at how different his life was from mine. At his knee I also learned some insights and aphorisms that I've heard repeated by other folk sages.

The kind of wise sayings I'm talking about are reflected in something I heard when I went to a birthday party for my friend Eddie Strother not long ago. I asked him if now, on his ninetieth birthday, he was planning to slow down and retire. He looked me straight in the eye, pursed his lips, and said: "Let me tell you something, boy. You rust out a lot quicker than you wear out."

On another occasion, I met one grand lady on a visit to Joplin, Missouri. We talked about many of the amazing things that had happened in her hundred years of life, from the invention of cars, to airplanes, the atom bomb, color television—and even men on the moon. I asked her what she considered the most significant thing that had happened in her great long life, and without batting an eye, she had it on the tip of her tongue: "Sonny, the greatest thing in my life has been R.F.D. mail!"

Who would have ever guessed that mail delivered to your door would stand above the other technological achievements of our time? Yet it was a simple, profound breakthrough.

It's a shame that, in America, we all too often cut ourselves off from our elders. My own experience suggests that older people have wonderful stories to tell; but too often, younger folks seem too preoccupied to focus on the rich past that can be opened up to them—and from them to us. I have noticed, though, that in rural communities, more than in urban areas, the generations still tend to do things together and enjoy each other's company. Everyone is richer for that experience, I'm sure.

As a matter of fact, I'm convinced that in the 1980s we're going to see a renewed respect for our elders—if for no other reason than because there are going to be so many of them around. With more and more people nowadays watching their health, not smoking, and maintaining good diets, more of us are going to lead healthy, extended lives. That's one reason I like to do my part to bridge the so-called age gap.

As I said earlier, one of my favorite bits on the "Today" show is to announce the birthdays of people who write in to say they are over 100 years old. The dozens of letters I receive each week often include some delightful message or remembrances of times gone by. One I especially enjoy was a letter written to me by a man who was about to turn 102 years old. In his scrawled handwriting, he explained, "I still like the girls, but I'm not sure why!"

Of course, old-timers have played a big part in my career and throughout my personal and family life. And it seems that just about everyone I meet has a story to tell about a favorite oldster in his own life. Here are some of mine.

Clown Hitchhiker

One day several years ago, I was doing an appearance as Bozo at a county fair in Maryland. On my way to the fair, however, my car ran out of gas. It was at least four miles to the next town, and I was stuck on a four-lane highway with cars just whizzing by.

There I was in my Bozo costume, my face all made up with a bulb nose and big, funny clown shoes, stranded in the middle of nowhere. So I got out of the car and started to walk. Unfortunately, as soon as I got a way down the road, it started to rain. The only choice I had was to try to hitchhike, and I thought I'd have no trouble getting a ride because every car that passed by was filled with kids on their way to the fair. For some reason, they all waved and honked their car horns—but no one stopped.

Soon, I was a mess. Makeup ran all over my face, my red clown-hair began to droop, and the costume got soaked right through. Finally, a disheveled old man in a 1947 Chevy pulled up alongside. There was no upholstery in the car, just springs, and the car smelled terrible. But just happy to get a ride, I wasn't about to complain. I jumped in, babbling along, telling him what happened. But he didn't say a word. In my wet clown getup, I must have been quite a sight.

When we got to the gas station four miles down the road, he let me out, and I thanked him profusely, practically kissing his feet. As I turned to leave, he spoke his first and only words:

"I know just how you feel, mister. Before I had my car, I used to hitchhike, and nobody would pick me up either."

Bar Bet

Bars and taverns seem to bring out the strangeness in people. If they're not telling tall tales, they may be playing "bar games," or even laying a friendly wager on a disputed point. But you shouldn't mess around unless you know the person you're dealing with.

In one bar a pompous, clothes-conscious young fellow was being awfully loud and disrespectful of the older patrons. He was bragging about how fine and expensive his skin-tight jeans were, especially compared to the old, baggy overalls worn by the other men. Finally, one old-timer had had enough.

"Young feller," the old man said, drawing out some playing cards and a large whip, "I'll bet you a glass of that wine you're drinking that if you lay this deck of cards on your leg, I can cut right through it with my whip and not even touch your pants."

"You're on—if you think you can see that far," the young man said.

With that, the old man cracked the whip with all his might, tore the young man's brand-new pants right off him, and left a bleeding welt on his leg.

"Barkeep," the old man said, "get that man some wine. I just lost myself a bet."

Getting Even

We often think of senior citizens as highly vulnerable. But sometimes they're not as helpless as we think. Several years ago I had stopped at a roadside cafe to learn that not a half-hour earlier a gang of motorcycle toughs had burst in. Apparently seeing an old man sitting at the counter, they decided to throw their weight around a bit.

First, one of the toughs took the old man's hamburger and ate it. Another drank the man's coffee, while another ate his slice of pie.

Throughout all this taunting, the old man didn't say a word. When the hoodlums were through, he got up and paid his check, and walked out silently.

The punk who had eaten the man's hamburger laughed derisively, and said to the waitress, "He sure wasn't much of a man, was he?"

"He's not much of a driver, either," said the waitress. "He must have run over six motorcycles getting out of the parking lot."

Public Speaking

Old-timers sometimes have a reputation for being a demanding, irascible bunch who want special treatment, especially when they're in a crowd. You can be sure, when I get to a more advanced age, I'm going to feel no qualms about doing a little demanding myself. After all, by that time, I'll have earned the right to a little more respect.

119

Curiously enough, old-timers show a bit of the same forth-rightness that I find so appealing in children. One night a number of years ago, there were fourteen of us having a special dinner in a fancy restaurant in town. Our neighbor, Old Man Weaver, joined us for the occasion, along with my now-departed dad and the rest of the family.

A mariachi band circulated around, going from table to table. It was a busy night, and there must have been 150 people in the restaurant. Nevertheless, when the band got around to our table, the music was too much to bear for Old Man Weaver.

He waved the band off furiously, and yelled at the top of his lungs, "Stop that blasted noise!"

Suddenly, you could have heard a pin drop in that place. "Thank you," Weaver said calmly, and sat down, as we all tried desperately to look as invisible as possible.

Speak Up

Governor Vic Atiyeh of Oregon told me that he was listening to a number of local politicos making speeches one day, when an old man stood in the back of the auditorium.

"Could you speak up, young feller?" the old man asked. "I can hardly hear you."

A woman at least ten years his senior then stood up from a seat near the front of the auditorium. "I can hear, all too well. Do you want to change places?"

Wave Goodbye

Sometimes, you just can't seem to please some old-timers. Governor Atiyeh went on to tell me that he heard about one older woman who was strolling along an Oregon beach with her young grandson. Suddenly, a giant wave swept over the beach, dragging the grandson out to sea.

The distraught older woman fell to her knees and prayed for her grandson's safe return, offering her own life instead. A few minutes later, another large wave returned the boy unharmed.

The woman looked the boy over carefully, and then turned her eyes skyward. "But he had a hat!"

High-Water Hogs

True to their proud and independent spirit, many old farmers have become rather sharp wheeler-dealers who usually get the best of a bargain. One old fellow in my town when I was a kid had a reputation for being a particularly shrewd businessman. He knew a good deal when he saw one, but he also knew when someone was trying to pull the wool over his eyes.

One day he went to see a piece of property in the next county that had been advertised for sale. It seemed to be a good enough parcel of land, but it was rather low and had a creek running across it. Moreover, the old-timer spotted what looked like high-water marks about five feet up on the trunks of some nearby trees. "It would appear that this land is flooded when that creek rises," he said to the owner.

"Oh, no," the owner assured him. "This property is never flooded. Those marks on those trees are where hogs have come up out of the bottoms and scraped the mud off their backs."

The old-timer mulled this over for a minute, and then said, "Well, I don't think I'm interested in the farm, but I'd sure like to buy some of those hogs."

Forgive and Forget

Sometimes advanced age brings evenhandedness as well as business acuity. Arkansas Governor Bill Clinton lost his bid for reelection in 1980, largely because he had pushed for an increase in the cost of automobile licenses. That turned out to be an extremely unpopular measure with the people.

When he began to test the waters in 1982 to see if he should make another try at the office, he ran into an old man in overalls who insisted he personally was responsible for Bill Clinton's defeat.

"I cost you eleven votes, you know. How many people do you think hurt you that bad?"

"I hope not too many," Bill Clinton replied.

"Well, I sure did. I got my whole family to vote against you."

"But why?"

"Had to. You raised the auto licenses. Cost me a fortune."

"Didn't you want your roads fixed?" the ex-governor persisted.

"Don't care," the old man said. "I sure didn't want to pay for it that way."

"Well, if I were to run for governor again, would you consider voting for me?"

The old man looked the politician up and down, and then smiled. "Yeah, we're even now."

Muleheadedness

Some of the wisest older folks I know have learned that one of the most important principles in life is knowing when to keep your mouth shut. One old farmer finally equipped himself with a new tractor to do his plowing, and he found himself with an old surplus mule on his hands. So he ran a notice in the paper advertising the mule for sale.

In a day or so, a city slicker came to the farm. He was interested in buying the mule for his weekend house. He was in such a hurry that he didn't ask any questions. He just paid the farmer and loaded the mule into the trailer.

The next day, the city slicker drove up hopping mad. "That mule is blind," he said. "I turned the animal out into a pasture, and the mule galloped headfirst into a tree! Then the mule got up and galloped into yet another tree!"

"Naw, mister," the farmer replied laconically. "That mule just don't give a damn."

Persuasive Argument

I don't go much for this idea of mandatory retirement. I know so many people who are still so bright and productive in their advanced years that it seems a shame to cut them off from their livelihood. Just because some people may be over sixty or older, you can't assume they're no longer able to do their jobs. On the contrary, they have a wealth of experience from which to draw. Some people may look forward to the day when they no longer have to work, but others continue to forge ahead—and they stay sharp as a tack and their integrity as well as their expertise seems to "age."

Governor Richard Riley of South Carolina told me about one oldster he heard about who was a circuit judge back in the days of Prohibition. When the judge was on his final week in a particular area, he would hear non-jury cases. Frequently, he would ask the lawyers to submit summaries of their positions and a copy of the relevant law to back them up.

One lawyer, trying to gain an upper hand on his adversary, knew that the old judge enjoyed a good drink now and then. So he delivered a half-gallon of the best bootleg whiskey he could find, along with his brief, to the judge.

Soon, the lawyer got a reply: "Dear Bill, I have read your brief and drunk your liquor. Your liquor was good, but your law was bad. I had to decide against you."

Cutting a Bargain

In a small town, some shopkeepers tend to stay around such a long, long time that they get to be fixtures in the community. Our local butcher has been in business as long as I can remember. He's getting on in years, and now he's got competition across the street. But his longevity on the block seems to have made him so secure that nothing will ruffle his feathers.

I overheard a woman shopper complaining to this butcher the other day about the price of his meat.

"Your pork chops are eighty-five cents a pound," she said. "Why, Dolan's Market, across the street, sells them for seventy cents a pound."

"Well," said the old butcher, "why don't you buy them from Dolan?"

"Because he's out of chops today, that's why," she retorted.

"Hah!" the butcher said. "When I'm out of chops, I price them at *fifty* cents a pound!"

Newfangled Gadgets

Some country folk I know are slow to change. Bound by tradition, they would rather do things the way they've always been done for generations, without a single alteration. This is especially true of the families who live in the hills, far away from towns and "civilization." Sometimes, it means they're a bit out of step with the rest of the world.

With all our gadgets and modern conveniences, we often take for granted such things as refrigerators. Way back in Colonial times, people used to store ice that had frozen on a nearby lake in specially insulated "ice houses." In this way, they could have ice well into the summer to use for refrigeration.

Even in my own childhood, I remember that a lump of ice could be a big treat. During the summer, the milkman used to come around in an ice-filled truck and deliver the milk in those old-fashioned glass bottles. Though each quart was topped off with about three inches of cream that settled in the neck of the bottle, the big thrill of the delivery wasn't the milk; it was the hunk of ice the milkman gave us to suck on and keep cool.

My grandmother's first fancy appliance was a refrigerator, and she immediately came up with some creative, down-home uses for it that the manufacturers never intended. For example, she made her own version of ice cream by whipping cream and strawberries together and freezing the mixture in the ice cube trays.

Her approach reminds me of a salesman who sold a refrigerator to an old farmer from a part of Kentucky I used to travel through. At the time, the area was so rural that even electricity was something of a novelty. A few weeks later, he found himself back in the same area, so he stopped off to see the farmer. "How do like that refrigerator I sold you?" he asked.

"Like it fine," said the farmer. "But it gives my missus a little trouble."

"How's that?" the salesman asked.

"She hasn't quite learned how to chop the ice into little squares to fit in the trays."

Campaign Curmudgeon

One thing's for sure, you can usually count on an old-timer to say what's on his mind.

Representative Ike Andrews, of North Carolina, told me that when he was campaigning, he got a big hello from an old fellow in a small rural town.

"Why you're Ike Andrews, aren't you!" the old man said.

"Yes, I am," Ike said, pleased at being recognized so quickly.

"You're running again, aren't you?"

"Certainly am," Ike said.

"Anybody running against you?"

"Not so far," Ike said. "I'm hoping I won't have any opposition this time."

"Oh, you got plenty of opposition," the old-timer said. "They just ain't filed yet."

Literally Speaking

Country folk are bound by tradition, to be sure. But they also tend to be true to their word—right down to the letter. In the old days, abiding by your word was a matter of honor—even in the most impossible circumstances.

On a wet, stormy night, a travelling salesman knocked at the door of a farmhouse seeking shelter. His knock was answered by the farmer who said yes, he could give the salesman a bed. The farmer showed him the stairs to the second floor, where the bedroom was located, and the salesman went off to sleep.

In the morning, he awoke to an unusual sight. The farmhouse was now surrounded by floodwaters, six feet deep. But as he looked out the window, something in the front yard arrested his attention. A straw hat was floating back and forth across the yard, from one side to the other. The salesman watched the hat's puzzling performance for several minutes, then called it to the attention of the farmer's daughter.

"Oh, that's grandpa," she explained after a moment. "He vowed he was going to mow the lawn today, come hell or high water."

Taking His Time

Whatever you do when talking to an old-timer, don't try to rush him. I learned long ago you can't get too pushy with old folks, and Senator Alan Cranston was reminded of this point during his bid for the Democratic Presidential nomination.

When he asked a weathered old New England farmer who seemed to be leaning his way for his support, the farmer just put things in perspective:

"Well, I take a long time making up my mind— even when I know what I'm going to do."

Chicken Feed

People who live close to the land seem to have a less frantic way of looking at life than the rest of the population. They enjoy poking fun at outsiders who presume to know more than they do about their method of working.

An efficiency expert watched as a farmer scattered feed around for his chickens. "Those chickens would feed faster if you put them in a smaller pen," he suggested.

"Yes, I suppose they would," the farmer agreed. "But what's a hen's time worth?"

Strawberries

An old man was working in the yard of a home for the elderly in a town near us in Virginia, when a farmer walked past with a wagonload of manure.

"Where are you going with that?" the old man asked.

"I'm gonna put it on my strawberries, if it's any of your business," the farmer snipped.

"You ought to be in here," the old man said. "They put sugar and cream on ours."

No News

One of the main traits of many old-timers is a wry sense of humor and an ability to see the funny side of some of our modern pastimes. Vaudeville performances typified the ability to laugh at ourselves—out loud and without restraint.

One old vaudeville routine that I heard when I first started working for NBC typifies the rural old-timer's laid-back attitude.

A man came back from a business trip and stopped in at the general store on his way home.

"Henry," he said to the old-timer who ran the store, "it's good to be home. Is there any news?"

Old Henry thought for a minute. "No," he finally said, "except your dog died."

"My dog died! What happened to my dog?"

"Well," Henry drawled, "your dog got ahold of the burnt horseflesh, and that's what killed him. Oher than that, though, there's no news."

"Horseflesh! Where'd my dog get horseflesh?"

"Well, your barn burned down, killing all the cows and the horses, and the dog went in and ate some of that burnt horseflesh, and that's what killed the dog. But other than that, there's no news."

"Wait. How did my barn burn down?"

"Well, apparently a spark flew over from the roof of your house."

"But what happened to the house?"

"Oh, boy, quite a fire. Sent sparks all over the area, and onto the barn, burning the barn down and killing all the livestock. The dog went right in and ate the horseflesh, and that's what killed him, I'm sure of that."

"How on earth did the house catch fire?"

"Well I'm sure it was from the candles. They must've caught on to the drapes or something, and started that whole house on fire, sending sparks . . ."

"But why were there candles in my modern home?"

"Well, you know, it was those candles that were around the coffin."

"What coffin?"

"I'm sorry to say, your mother-in-law died."

"But she was young, and in perfect health! What could she have died from."

"Well, rumor has it around the neighborhood it was the shock of your wife running away with the milkman. But outside of that, there ain't no real news around here."

Home Brew

One sure way of making a living in the hill country was to manufacture some private moonshine. I know some of my ancestors were alcohol entrepreneurs.

One city dweller was travelling up in the mountains of North Carolina, near where my family used to live, and stopped at a gas station. An old guy comes up with a jug over his shoulder and a big rifle, and says to the city slicker, "How'd you like some corn whiskey?"

"No, thanks. I'm in a hurry."

With that, the old mountain man put a shotgun to the man's head. "Drink the whiskey," he demanded.

Having no choice, the driver sniffed the jug, made a face, and then gulped down a mouthful. It had to be the worst thing he had ever tasted, and he did all he could to keep from gagging. After he stopped reeling, he mopped the sweat from his brow.

"Now, here," said the old mountain man. "Hold the gun on me."

Feed Store

Another old-timer ran a feed store, but he wasn't making any money. The store just kept going downhill, more and more, until he finally thought he was going to have to close. But he decided to take a gamble and invest $50—a lot of money in those days—in a thousand baby chicks that he bought from a salesman.

The neighbors all did their share of clucking about how this poor guy couldn't make it in the feed business, so now he was going to try to sell chickens.

But instead of selling the chicks, this fellow decided on a totally different strategy. During the months of February and March, he ran an Easter bonus: Every customer who came into the store got ten free chicks.

Now, his neighbors thought that he'd gone completely mad. Here his feed business was about to fail, and he was giving away freebies.

By Easter, however, he was riding high once again. In fact, his business had tripled. Each of his former customers who got the free chicks, it seems, now came back again and again—to buy a lot more feed—to nourish their growing brood.

Squeezing a Profit

Not all old folks are astute at book-learning, but that doesn't mean they aren't shrewd at business. One good old Southern boy from Texas ran a steakhouse with his elderly father. It was a place I used to eat at occasionally, just a little steakhouse, and the meat really wasn't all that good. But the company was nice and the owners apparently made a few bucks.

One day, the son was talking to a friend about the business, and I just couldn't help overhearing.

"I keep tellin' dad we should raise our prices. But my dad says we're gettin' by, 'cause we're buying steaks for a dollar and we sell them for three. I guess he's right—we should be happy with that three percent profit."

Eyewitness

Out in the country, you can't always expect older folks to give you a straight answer to your questions. Sometimes, they seem to have a better way of getting their points across.

One time, a car came barreling down a road and failed to negotiate a curve. It shot off the road and struck a tree, injuring the driver and a passenger.

Shortly, a police officer arrived at the scene, and he started questioning witnesses.

"Did you see what happened?" the officer asked an old farmer toward the front of the crowd.

"Well," said the man slowly, "from where I was standing, it looked like that fellow was trying to get eighty miles out of a ten-mile stretch of road."

Southern Woodsman

In the old days there were many people who knew how to make a living off the land. Free from answering a boss's whims, they formed the basis of the American tradition of self-sufficiency. Sometimes I like to muse about what life must have been like in those days. The old-timers who lived in the area where I grew up told stories that shed some light on a way of life that today is largely forgotten.

Many years ago, the Ouachita River, a river that meanders through several Southern states, was navigable for much of its length. Along the banks of the Ouachita, in those days, there lived an old woodsman named Primus Washington. Primus eked out a slender living hunting and fishing and trapping, and selling part of whatever he killed or caught. One day, he was especially lucky and caught a very large raccoon.

Steamboats still plied the river in those days, and Primus hailed one, to try to sell his prize. When the captain of the boat found out that he had been stopped, not for a passenger, as he had thought, but by Primus trying to sell a raccoon, he got blistering mad and gave the old man a tongue lashing. Primus listened quietly from his place on the river bank, nodding from time to time, apparently in agreement.

"Given a choice," the captain declared as he ended his tirade, "I'd rather eat a piece of dogmeat before I'd eat a piece of your damned raccoon!"

Primus stood scratching his head for a long moment, then replied thoughtfully, "Well, cap, I guess it's owing to what you're used to."

Courting Disaster

A man was on trial for murder, and the tide seemed to be running against him, so he tried to bribe an elderly juror to hold out for a verdict of manslaughter. The jury was out for three, four, five, six days, and the accused man's load of anxiety was nearly unbearable. But in the end, the jury brought in a verdict of manslaughter.

"Did you have much trouble getting the others to vote for manslaughter?" the man asked the old juror.

"You bet I did," the man replied. "They all wanted to vote for acquittal."

The Hole Truth

In another court case, an old farmer was giving testimony that was so far fetched that the judge thought it best to warn him that he was in serious danger of perjuring himself.

"Are you aware," the judge asked, "of what will happen to you if you are caught lying under oath?"

"When I die I'll go to hell," the old man replied.

"Yes, but what else?" the judge asked.

The old man was puzzled for a moment. "You mean there's more?"

IX

SNAKE OIL

tore-bought prescriptions and scientific medical practice may be important advances in a "civilized" culture, but I certainly hope we never lose the old-fashioned folk remedies that were so much fun—and may well have done more good than highfalutin physicians acknowledge.

Actually, my favorite part of the old "snake oil" tradition, apart from the fast-talking salesmen, is the fact that some of the folk remedies provide me with an excuse to eat more. You see, all the down-home schools of medical wisdom concur that the level of a person's food intake is a strong clue to the health of his body—and I certainly wouldn't want to give anybody the impression that I'm not feeling up to par. I really didn't mind being sick when I was young, though. That gave my mother a reason to fix me a "special" loose poached egg with toast and bacon bits, a treat that she said wouldn't upset my stomach.

On the other hand, the Willard Scott Medical Handbook states emphatically that when a person loses his appetite completely, it's a sure sign that something serious is wrong. I have rarely been so sick that I couldn't eat, but you can be sure that on those occasions there was bound to be some sort of a tasty home remedy in grandmother's closet to cure whatever ailed me.

Of course, I realize doctors are necessary. In fact, some of my best friends are doctors. But for me, a doctor's good word is the best prescription of all. When I'm feeling lousy, it's worth twice the doctor's fee just to find out that everything's fine and I'll be okay soon.

For centuries, doctors depended almost exclusively upon the body to heal itself. In fact, before such things as antibiotics came onto the scene, many of the medicines they prescribed were totally useless in fighting disease.

There were all kinds of strange concoctions that they developed, most of which only served to reassure the patient that something was being done for them. Unfortunately, in the drive toward more modern medications, we've tended to dismiss some of the old remedies, which, despite the odd ingredients, actually worked. Many of these drugs were combinations of herbs and other plants that really had some healing properties.

It even seems that with some of these preparations, we've started to come full circle. Originally, most medicines originated from plants. With all our modern technology, we have tended to discard these old remedies. Instead, we have developed some snazzy medications, and given them fancy scientific names.

Now, however, there is a move back toward "generic" drugs, where people can buy the actual drug compounded without the fancy brand-name. The oddest part of all this is that many of these drug compounds are often composed of the same ingredients that can be found in—you guessed it—plant and herbal home remedies.

Looking back in our own history, there are a few instances where home remedies were notable. In Colonial days, when Captain John Smith was exploring the Chesapeake and Potomac waters, he was reportedly stung by a poisonous stingray. From what I've read, the Indians saved his life—and it wasn't Pocahontas this time—by packing around the wound a certain type of mud that can be found in the riverbed. Although Smith could have been killed by the venom, this special mud drew out the poison, and the swelling subsided.

I've even had some personal experiences with these home remedies. I had an Uncle Dave Phillips, an old doctor down in Texas, who was getting a little senile as he entered his eighties. He moved up to my grandmother's farm in Maryland to spend his retirement. That way we could keep our eyes on him so he wouldn't get into trouble. After all, he didn't have all his faculties.

Some days he was brighter than others—just like you and me, I suppose. One time, he developed a terrible rash on his ankle, and grandma carted him around to four different specialists who couldn't find any way to cure it. It persisted for weeks, until, on one of his more lucid days, he told my Uncle Paul, "Take me outside."

They walked into the woods near the farm, and Uncle Dave dug a little something out of the ground. He brought it back into the house, shaved it, boiled it, and soaked it for a while. Afterwards, he poured the soupy mixture onto a cloth, and wrapped it around his ankle. In a couple of days, the rash totally cleared up.

I never found out what kind of root that was, but it proved to me that some of these old ways were worth remembering. For a mild sore throat, I used to be given horehound candy and molasses, which actually coated the throat like modern cough medicine. As I got older, I used to dress it up in an adult version: I added a little whiskey.

But one "cure" I'll never forget was something my grandmother used to call an "assifidity bag," for whenever I had a *bad* sore throat. This bag was a little sack stuffed with onions, herbs, dried mushrooms, garlic—you name it. If anything smelled awful and strong, it could be found in there. Anyway, this whole concoction was wrapped with a mustard plaster around the front of my neck. I have no idea if it ever really worked, but I can tell you the stink was so bad that no one else would get close enough to catch my sore throat from me!

Here are some other ticklish stories that I remember about medicines and doctors.

Maintaining Health

With many of their herbal remedies, our ancestors apparently had the right idea. But some people "way back when" had questionable theories about how the body could be kept in fine health. One such theory, which I came across years ago, goes like this:

"A daily bath, shower or otherwise, is a modern invention, devised to sell bath-tubs. I personally have known but two men who acknowledge to a daily shower bath every day. One of them died of chronic diarrhoea, the other was a hydropathist, a great stout, raw-boned six footer. He was always bathing, and was always sick; he would frequently douse himself in cold water two or three times a day. Does any reader of mine know any old man who has been a daily cold-water bather all his days, or even for any five years of his life? When a man is not well, bathing of some kind is advisable under certain circumstances, but it should not be continued; as soon as he is well he ought to stop."

(Originally from Dr. W. W. Hall, *The Guide-Board to Health, Peace and Competence; or the Road to Happy Old Age* [1869].)

Dirt-Eating Cure

Believe it or not, in areas of the South it is not uncommon for some people to occasionally eat dirt! It's a tradition that has passed from generation to generation, and exists today as a way to "clean out the system." These people may believe it helps them (sort of an internal sandblasting), but even in the old days, most people saw that it was the kind of unhealthy practice that ought to be discouraged.

Some people say the practice originated with the American Indians, although others point to Africa as the place where it started. Wherever it began, apparently the Indians had been known to overdo it—whatever the digestive pluses of eating dirt it's got to be murder on the teeth—so the following sure cure for dirt abuse was devised specifically for them. After I read it, I had no doubt that it works. The secret ingredient: A bat, or rearmouse. Here are the specifics:

> The Indian children are much addicted to eat dirt, and so are some of the Christians. But roast a bat on a skewer, then pull the skin off, and make the child that eats dirt, eat the roasted rearmouse; and he will never eat dirt again. This is held as an infallible remedy.*

---

* From TAR HEEL LAUGHTER by Richard Walser. Copyright The University of North Carolina Press 1974. Used by permission of the publisher.

Second Opinion

Many times when people go to the doctor, they really don't need medicines—just a kind word. However, when the patients are not so kind even a doctor can give them a dose of their own medicine.

In the waiting room at my doctor's office the other day, I overheard the doctor as his patient was about to leave.

"You've really got to lose some weight," the doctor said. "You'll feel a lot better if you lose fifteen or twenty pounds."

The woman was extremely indignant at hearing this. "Are you implying that I'm overweight?" she asked.

"Well, yes," the doctor replied, "I guess I am."

"Then you must be some kind of quack," she snapped, "and I'd like a second opinion."

"Okay," said the doctor, "you're also very ugly!"

Woman Doctor

A friend of mine who had just taken a new job was sent by his company for a required physical examination. He arrived at the doctor's office and was told by a receptionist to go into the next room, take off his clothing, and wait. The doctor would be along shortly, she said.

The man waited for a few minutes. Then there was a knock at the door. "Come in," he called.

The door opened and a woman walked in. "It's all right," she said, as the man reached for his trousers. "I'm the doctor."

She gave him a very thorough examination, and then said, "You're in good shape. Do you have any questions?"

"Just one," the man said. "Why did you knock?"

More Than a Mouthful

A man went to see his doctor and told him that he had swallowed a horse. Realizing that such delusions can be dangerous, the doctor said, "Okay, I'll operate at once and remove it."

The man was then wheeled into the operating room, and as soon as he had been anesthetized, the doctor had a horse brought in. When the man woke up, the doctor said, "Everything's all right now. We've removed this horse from your stomach."

"No, that's not the one," said the man. "That horse is black. The one I swallowed was white."

Kickapoo Indian Sagwaw

While researchers scramble about for a cure for the common cold—don't ask me why; I cured it myself way back in Chapter 1—remedies of one sort or another have been available for generations. Here are three that I've found to be most common in backwoods areas:

- Some people suggest drinking a variety of medicinal teas: coltsfoot, peppermint, yarrow, boneset, mint, catnip, verbena, horehound, and sage.

- If for no other reason, I love one black and syrupy cold mixture for its name. Many years ago, it was sold commercially as: "Kickapoo Indian Sagwaw." Whoever made it included these ingredients: horehound, anise, checkerberry, sarsaparilla, camomile, wormwood.

- Whatever commercial remedies for the sniffles become available these days, in some parts of the country, doctors of the old school still recommend eating garlic, as well as various mixtures of licorice and lemon.

Hungarian Hat Trick

Dosages of these cold cures vary according to the doctor (if your "doctor" happens to be your grandmother, proceed with extra caution!), the severity of the illness, and the age of the sufferer. Sometimes, you can't tell how much is "enough."

One of the strangest dosages for a cold remedy that I ever heard of was included in the cure known as the "Hungarian Hat Trick." If you suffer from a cold, first place a hat on your bedpost. Then, according to this remedy, get into bed and start drinking. When you see two hats, discontinue use.

Dog Food

My former neighbor Clarence had an awful skin rash on his face, so he went to the doctor and was given a whole battery of allergy tests. Afterwards, the doctor told him he had a rare allergy. Moreover, the doctor said, the only known treatment was to eat a certain combination of ingredients that could be found only in dog food.

"You have to eat a can a day for thirty days," the doctor said, "and the entire problem will clear up."

Well, the guy thought this advice was looney, but he agreed. He went to the supermarket and got a supply of dog food, his wife prepared it in salads and casseroles, and even hid some in the meat loaf. Sure enough, his face began to clear up.

On the twenty-ninth day, however, he died. Hysterical, the wife called up the doctor to tell him the news.

"But what happened?" the doctor said. "Did he have a heart attack or something?"

"No, No," the widow cried. "Clarence was sitting on the couch licking his paws, and he fell off and broke his neck."

Health Insurance

Grandmother Scott always used to say that the best way to maintain your health was to find a doctor who was interested in keeping you well—not just in treating you when you were sick. That reminds me of the old Chinese tradition of paying the family doctor when you're feeling good, but giving him nothing at all when you're under the weather.

A friend of my grandmother's, old Mrs. Hickey, had already outlived two town dentists. Obviously, her longevity was directly related to her smarts because she was careful to put this Chinese theory into practice during her first visit to the young Doctor Dentyne. She absolutely hated any degree of pain, so she saw to it that it was in the dentist's best interest to go easy.

Mrs. Hickey, a sweet, frail woman, about eighty-five years old, hobbled slowly into the dentist's chair. After washing his hands, Dr. Dentyne greeted the old woman in his best chairside manner. "Good afternoon, Mrs. Hickey. Are you ready to begin the examination?"

"Oh, yes, doctor," she said sweetly. Then, reaching out as quick as lightning, she grabbed the doctor in his *most* vulnerable area and said, "Now, we're not going to hurt each other, are we, doctor?"

Lame Excuses

When a child is absent from school, the teacher always asks for a letter of explanation from his parents. Most of the time the child has a routine illness, but some excuse letters that I've seen from parents are pretty lame themselves.

Here are a few that I borrowed from Bob Best, who operates the *News Progressive.* He, in turn, filched it from the Mt. Carroll New York *Democrat,* which had received it from a Savannah corporation correspondent, who had clipped it from a newspaper down South. Remember, these are parent-written excuses, unedited and uncensored:

- Dear School: Please excuse Jim for being absent on Jan. 28, 29, 30, 31, 32, and 33rd. Jim have a acre in his side.

- Jane could not come to school today, she was bothered by *very close* veins.

- Joe has been absent because he had two teeth taken out of his face.

- Please excuse Hazel. She has been sick and under the doctor.

- I kept Suzie home because she had to go Christmas shopping, because I didn't know what size she wear.

- My son is sick and under the doctor's care and should not physical education. Please execute him.

- Linda was absent from school because she had a going-over.

- Please excuse Esther from physical education for a few days. She fell out of a tree yesterday and misplaced her hip.

- Please excuse Jack for being out Friday. He had loose vowels.

- Please excuse June from gym. She is administrating.

- Harold was absent yesterday because he was playing football and was hurt in the growing part.

- My daughter was absent yesterday because she was tired. She spent the weekend with the Marines.

- Please excuse Randall for being. It was his father's fault.

- Cindy was absent Dec. 11–15 because she had a fever, sore throat, headache, upset stomach. Her sister was also sick: Fever, sore throat, headache. Her mother has a low-grade temperature and aches all over. I won't feelin' the best either. Sore throat and fever. There must be flu going on. Her father also got hot last night.

X

MELTING POT

I've often heard people say that the only true Americans were the original inhabitants of these lands—the Indians. Other than the Indians, we're a nation of immigrants. We've seen an incredible mixture of people arriving on these shores to make themselves a new home, and each new group has made its own indelible impression on the American culture.

It hasn't been easy going for all of these people, of course. Often they arrive without much money, they may speak no English, and many find it difficult to get along. But after a while, it seems, most people find their way to build a better world for themselves and their children.

But it takes time to blend into a society. Sometimes, it takes generations. Even then, we remain a nation of groups. We have

Italian-Americans, Hispanic-Americans, Polish-Americans, Irish-Americans, German-Americans, Afro-Americans, and Russian-Americans—literally hundreds of different groups of people who consciously strive to maintain some kind of a tie to their original heritage, while at the same time staking their claim as true Americans. We are rightfully proud of our cultural and ethnic identities, and it's wonderful to be able to explore our national origins and celebrate our diversity.

Some people say they can tell a person's national origin by the way he looks, talks, and acts—no matter how long his family has been in America. I'm really not so sure.

Southerners of any ethnic background may pepper their conversation with "Bless your heart," and New Englanders, no matter what their nationalities, may utter an occasional "Ahyup."

On the other hand, some regional conversational quirks clearly have ethnic roots. For example, when I first started travelling around different regions of the country, I noticed that many people in the Upper Plains States around the Great Lakes would often automatically acknowledge points in conversation by saying, "You betcha," or sometimes just "You bet." It finally dawned on me that this was probably a language peculiarity that had survived from those people's Swedish and Norwegian heritage. In those early days in the U.S., the people would say, "Ya, sure, you betcha," in a sort of broken English—and a version of that response apparently remains intact today.

All our various national identities have given us a wealth of amusing stories that play upon—and explode—notions of national characteristics. I don't mean to single out any particular group as the butt of a funny story. In fact, these stories are really universal. They prove that no matter how different we appear at first, we all really have a lot in common. Here are a few that I like to spin.

Weather Wizard

When we're speaking of "national characteristics," American Indians are one group often thought by people to have special knowledge of nature and the elements that the rest of us do not possess. Through centuries-old traditions, they have developed a "hot line" to the forces of nature.

One Westerner told me that he lived near an Indian reservation, and he learned to rely on the Indians to find out the weather. He swore by their astonishing accuracy. Every time he ran into the old chief, this guy would ask, "What's the weather going to be, Chief?"

The chief would answer, "Going to rain today," or "Going to be sunny all week." Incredibly, the chief was usually right on the money.

One cloudy day the man again asked the chief, "What kind of weather are we going to have today?"

"Don't know," the chief answered. "Radio broke."

Sure Sign

Another old Indian was once predicting a terrible winter. He forecast, "Gray skies, many clouds come and bring great snowfall. Hard winter ahead."

When asked how he knew all this, he replied, "White man gather much firewood."

Indian Trail Expert

Some vacationers at a dude ranch out West were riding horseback one day when they came upon an Indian lying on a dirt road with his ear to the ground. Amused, they stopped their horses and walked over to the Indian. The old Indian glanced at them and said, "Wagon down road about two miles. Pulled by two horses. Matched set, dappled gray. Man in wagon, woman in wagon. Woman wearing bonnet, flowered dress."

"That's amazing!" one tourist said, astounded. "He can tell all that by listening to the ground."

The Indian looked up at them once again, and grunted, "No, ran over me twenty minutes ago."

Language Lapse

In my many trips across the country for the "Today" show, I have seen that we are indeed a land of many peoples. I love the fact that in our large cities there are vast pockets of ethnic groups that retain much of their original cultures. For instance, many cities have their own Chinatowns or Little Italys, which are entire worlds unto themselves.

What is most surprising about these ethnic pockets is that—especially with members of the older generation—English seems to remain a second language.

Senator Quentin Burdick of North Dakota told me that when he was campaigning for reelection not long ago, he spent some time in the "German part" of his state. When he met one little old lady who was sporting a *babushka* on her head, he held out his hand and introduced himself.

"Hi, I'm Senator Burdick, and I'm running for reelection . . ."

"Vas?" she replied.

"I said, I'm Senator Burdick," he repeated somewhat louder.

"Who?"

"Senator Burdick," he said, straining to make himself understood. "I'm Senator Burdick."

"Senator Burdick!" she said as her face lit up with recognition. "My, oh my, Senator Burdick, you know this is the first time I have seen you alive!"

Change of Heart

The Irish certainly take their politics seriously. And when it comes to choosing sides of an issue, they usually stick with their choice permanently. In the supermarket before a recent election, I overheard two women speaking with heavy Irish accents.

"Have you heard the news?" one said. "Sean O'Reilly has become a Republican."

"Certainly, it can't be!" the other cried. "Why, I just saw him at Mass last Sunday."

Speaking His Mind

One thing about the Irish, they're not afraid to let you know exactly *how* they feel, *whenever* they feel like it.

I've heard that when Theodore Roosevelt was the Republican candidate for president, he gave a speech on a crowded New York street one day. But he was constantly interrupted by a bois-terous—but proud—Irishman.

"I'm a Democrat! I'm a Democrat!" the Irishman repeated loudly.

Roosevelt finally confronted the man. "Exactly why, sir, are you a Democrat?" he asked.

"Me grandfather was a Democrat, me father was a Demo-crat, and I am also a Democrat," the Irishman said.

"Now tell me, my friend," Roosevelt said testily, "suppose your grandfather had been a jackass, and your father had been a jackass, what would you be then?"

"To be sure," said the Irishman, "a Republican."

Irish Drivers

A friend of ours had just returned from a month-long stay in Ireland, so Mary and I invited him to spend the weekend with us out at the farm. We picked him up at the airport, and on the way back, I took a country road that I used as the "scenic route."

It's a lovely drive, but it burns me up when I find myself behind a slow-moving car or truck that I can't pass. It didn't help, either, when my friend started to laugh. But apparently, he'd had the same thing happen to him in Ireland.

You see, he told us, the roads in Ireland are frequently narrow and winding, with high banks on both sides, which makes passing difficult, and at times, downright impossible. On just such a road, he found himself behind a car that was barely crawling. He tooted his horn to alert the driver, a woman, that he was behind her and in something of a hurry. But she didn't increase her speed, so he leaned on his horn rather angrily.

Her response to this was to stick her head out the window and yell back at him, "Pig! Pig! Dirty pig!"

This incensed our friend, and as soon as he came to a wide enough place to pass, he pulled up by the woman and yelled, "Cow! Cow! Fat cow!"

And he ran smack into the pig.

Lighter Note

Over that same weekend, our friend told us that like residents in rival American states, Irish counties frequently engage in some verbal sparring. For instance, residents of County Kerry, in Ire-. land, are frequently the butt of other people's jokes—especially jokes told by people from County Cork. While he was in a pub in County Cork, our friend heard what he says is a perfect example of the rivalry.

A recently arrived priest, at a parish in Kerry, wanted to buy a new chandelier for the church. One of his flock got up to speak in opposition to the proposal, however.

"Father," he began, "I'm against it for three reasons. First of all, there's nobody within five miles of the church who can spell chandelier. Secondly, there's nobody within ten miles who can play one. And thirdly, what we need most of all in here is more light."

Irish Toasts

- I hope you are all here to do honor to the toast. As many of ye as is present will say "Here!" and as many of ye as is not present will say "Absent!"

- May you live all the days of your life.

- May good fortune follow you all your days—and never catch up with you.

Irish Wake

Boston is a great Irish city, and visiting the Irish pubs there by the waterfront makes me feel as close to being in Ireland as any place in America. The people in the crowded bars speak with more than just a touch of Irish in their accents, and an extra measure of blarney in their stories.

On one Boston trip, I heard in one of these pubs the outrageous story of a popular local character, Tommy O'Grady, who had recently died. When Tommy passed away, it filled his friends with grief, so there was no shortage of mourners to attend his wake. A robust drinker, Tommy was toasted again and again by his friends and family. But, by and by, the supply of stout and porter ran out, so it was decided that the mourners would repair to this local pub to finish out the night.

"But what about Tommy?" somebody asked. "We can't just go off and leave him here."

Everybody agreed that this was true, so they decided to take him along with them. They propped him up on a bar stool and proceeded to enjoy themselves.

Presently a stranger approached Tommy. "Can you give me a light for me pipe?" the stranger asked courteously. Tommy, of course, made no reply.

"I said will you give me a match for me pipe?" the stranger repeated, a bit louder, somewhat miffed at the lack of response. Still, though, there wasn't a word.

Angered, the stranger grabbed Tommy by the shirt front. "I'll teach you to be civil to a stranger who means you no harm," he said roughly. And with that, he punched the cold corpse in the mouth.

Naturally, it fell to the floor, turning over a couple of bar stools in the process, and causing a great clatter.

Tommy's friends looked around from their revels, aghast. "What happened?" somebody finally asked.

"I had to do it, lads," the stranger explained. "He pulled a knife on me."

Blarney Stone

Whenever I go someplace new, I always want to see the local sights. But I often try to keep in mind that as a guest in a new town or in a foreign country, I have to be on my best behavior. Sometimes "tourist" can be a dirty word.

One group of American tourists I heard about arrived in Ireland and engaged a guide to show them the sights. But they were a hard group to please and found fault with nearly everything: either the weather was either too hot or too cold, or too rainy or too dry; or prices were too high, and the natives were rude. Nothing, it seemed, was right. Then, to top it off, when they arrived at Blarney Castle, it was closed.

"This is the last straw," said a woman who had been the

main complainer in the group. "We've come all this distance, and now we can't kiss the Blarney Stone."

"Well, now," said their guide, not unsympathetically. "You know that if you kiss someone who has kissed the Blarney Stone, it's the same as kissing the Stone itself."

"Why, I didn't know that," said the woman, hope dawning in her face. "And have you kissed it?"

With a wicked gleam in his eye, the guide responded, "Even better. I sat on it."

Communication Gap

It's bad enough when you are a stranger in a country and you can speak the language. But if you *don't* know the language, you spend half your time guessing what people are telling you. Most the time, I'm sure, they have no idea what *you're* saying, either.

My friend Tracy, who recently retired, decided to spend his newfound leisure time traveling, since he had never gone out of the United States in his life. He embarked on his first ocean voyage, and at dinner the first night out he found himself seated across the table from a Frenchman. Before starting to eat, the Frenchman stood up and said, *"Bon appetit."*

Tracy rose, bowed, and said, "Tracy."

The next morning at breakfast, the Frenchman rose once again, bowed, and said, *"Bon appetit."*

Tracy rose, bowed, and said, "Tracy."

After breakfast, someone took Tracy aside and told him that the Frenchman was not introducing himself, but saying "Enjoy your meal."

"Oh, is that all?" said Tracy. The next morning, he arose, bowed, and said, *"Bon appetit."*

And the Frenchman rose, bowed, and said, "Tracy."

War Horse

There are a lot of put-down stories that make the rounds, in which the nationality or origin of the characters is interchangeable. I don't like put-down jokes as a rule, but sometimes they really shouldn't offend anybody. Here's one that I like to tell, because I never heard of anyone who said he was offended by it.

Two Cossacks in the army of the Czar had a problem that seemed beyond their ability to solve. They couldn't tell their new horses apart. First, they tried clipping the mane on one, and leaving the other unclipped. This worked for a while, but in time, the mane grew back, and they were confronted with the same old problem. Next, they tried clipping the tail of one horse, with the same result: it worked for a time, but eventually, the tail grew back.

Then one of the soldiers hit on the perfect solution. "Let's measure them," he exclaimed one day. They did, and sure enough, the black horse was two inches taller than the white horse.

XI

LOVEBIRDS

hen it comes to personal relationships, we've certainly made progress in the past twenty years—calling it a sexual revolution is probably an understatement.

Still, some things never change. When I was first starting to date, I wanted really to impress the girls I was with, just like any boy today does. But I was a little rough-hewn, not exactly "Mr. Suave" all the time, and so I made my share of social mistakes. As the saying goes, "You can take the boy out of the country, but you can't take the country out of the boy."

I took one date to a beautiful spot on the banks of the Potomac. There, we set up a gorgeous picnic, complete with fine champagne, and fancy cheeses from a specialty shop—they cost me a fortune! I, of course, was button-burstingly proud of myself for being so sophisticated. I just knew this girl was going to be impressed. We sat watching the boats sail by, with the wind blowing gently across the water, and I felt like a Continental lover. Just as we started to get a little amorous, though, some dust blew into my face, and I sneezed and broke wind—loudly— at the same time. It's hard to kick off any kind of serious relationship on that kind of note.

But as I see it, more and more people are returning to more traditional values. There are some important, practical reasons for maintaining just one mate, beyond legitimate concerns about health and longevity. I think a lot of people are getting just plain tired of flings and exploring their fantasies, and now things are beginning to settle down.

To me, there's no substitute for a marriage based on fidelity, and trust, and respect. Of course, things may never return to the way they used to be, with sex before marriage an absolute taboo. We'd just be deluding ourselves to say that there hasn't been a long-lasting loosening up in our overall outlook on these matters. But as interest in long-term relationships begins to grow once again, more and more of our younger people will find that respect for one another—love is the center of true happiness.

Even as we show reverence for moral value, however, we can still appreciate the silly side of love and sex. It's not my intention to be ribald or lewd in the stories that follow. I'm just not interested in that. But I *am* interested in those lighter things in life that make us laugh.

For instance, many girls in my generation were not allowed to go out with any boy who owned a Nash. Their mothers felt that any boy who drove a Nash was up to no good. How did the mothers of America get that impression? All the Nash-owning sons of America had to do was push a button and the front seat went down!

But even as I chuckle at courtship rituals I realize that, underlying the fun and silliness, is a very serious issue—shoring up the strength of the family unit. I don't really understand the "modern" practice of "marry today, divorce tomorrow." Of course, not all marriages are going to be successful; some people are going to stray, and some will naturally grow apart after a number of years. But I feel that kids should be encouraged to look for a mate with lifelong potential and taught to give marriage their best shot.

How do you help make a marriage last? Here's how Mary gave our partnership her best shot not too long ago. She and I had a heck of an argument recently about some minor point, and we didn't speak for a full day. On the second day, as the silence continued she decided to water the garden. As I walked past, she turned the hose on me, drenching my clothes. Well, that broke the ice, and all was forgiven. Though I don't even recall what the argument was about, I do remember our laughing together, long and hard. Incidents like this one convince me that mixing love with a sense of humor will do wonders in keeping our families and nation together.

Lucky or Knot

Sex before marriage is not exclusively a product of today's society, of course. In the old days, shotgun weddings were sometimes the solution when the bride *had* to get married. Other answers to the question of premarital sex had a similar American flavor.

For instance, back in New England in the 1800s, when a boy would come to see a young girl of marrying age, the family wanted to ensure them of some privacy without taking too many chances. It was so cold in that region during the winter that even a fireplace didn't offer much heat. So the only way the two young lovers could converse would be to lie down together in a wooden bed with loads of warm covers over it.

Now, if that wasn't a ready invitation for hanky-panky, I don't know what is. But the families in New England were awfully clever. The wooden bed was fitted with a board, that slipped directly in between the two lovers to keep them from touching. This meeting, after all, was strictly for talking.

Occasionally, though, I've heard an eager young couple might see to it that the board had a convenient knothole.

Lean Pickings

When the knot is finally tied, however, men sometimes don't get all the support they might like from their spouses.

Governor James Hunt of North Carolina told me that a few years ago, his wife got a call from a local civic leader for some biographical information. It seems that Governor Hunt had been selected as the organization's Man of the Year.

"Well," Mrs. Hunt told him over the phone. "That just shows what kind of year it's been."

Rude Awakening

There was a man I knew in West Virginia who had been rather unlucky in his relationships. His wife had run off, leaving him to raise his son by himself. The man decided to spare his boy the same pain, so he raised the youngster without ever letting him see a woman.

When the boy was twenty-one, the father took him to town for the first time, and before long, they saw three pretty women walking toward them.

"What are those, dad?" asked the boy.

"Those are geese," the father replied.

That night, when the two were back at their isolated homestead, the boy said, "Dad, I'd sure like to go back and see that tallest goose again."

Up in Smoke

My friend Murphy told me that one time, while visiting his friend Bert, he noticed an urn, about half full of ashes, on the mantle. "What are these?" Murphy asked.

"My wife's ashes," Bert replied.

Murphy replaced the lid gently. "Oh, I'm sorry," he said sympathetically. "I didn't know your wife had passed away."

"She hasn't," said Bert. "She smokes a pipe."

Hotel Honeymoon

A teacher of mine back in junior high school used to yell at me whenever I started fooling around with the girls: "Willard! Don't bother with girls until you get educated and have something to offer!"

I didn't like that too much at the time, but she did have a point. There's a lot more involved in any solid relationship than just sex. The young girls, too, were coached in this principle by their mothers, who said, "No man will buy the cow when he can get the milk for free."

It may seem old fashioned, but I can see now that there are many reasons for a couple to hold out until marriage—not the least of which is to have a special moment to savor and cherish before the responsibilities of marriage and family become a factor. My first night as a husband was one to remember, in more ways than one.

Mary and I drove right from our reception to a lovely resort in Hot Springs, Virginia. As we checked in, we tried not to look too conspicuous—though that was pretty hard when handfuls of rice started spilling out of my coat pocket. Anyway, the clerk at the desk assigned us a beautiful bridal suite, and I felt as if I was riding on top of the world.

Mary went into the bathroom to get ready for dinner, and I flopped back on the bed for a brief rest. But I flopped so hard that the bed collapsed. Mary rushed out, nervously laughing about the whole thing, and we called housekeeping to ask for a new bed. "But you've just been there five minutes," they protested.

Anyway, they sent a maintenance man up, and when he arrived, he looked at Mary and me like he couldn't believe his eyes. A smile crept over his face, and he gave me a knowing look which said: "Mmmmm, what a man!"

Overstaying a Welcome

At least on our honeymoon, I didn't have the problem of one young couple I know. They had been married for exactly six months, and in honor of the occasion, his new bride fixed his favorite dinner, complete with fine wine and candlelight.

After dinner, they were seated in front of the fireplace, sipping brandy. "Darling," she said, snuggling up to him. "Now that we've been married six months, don't you think your mother could find another place to stay?"

The man looked at her, astonished.

"*My* mother? I thought she was *your* mother!"

Parents' Disapproval

There's a lot more straight talk these days between men and women, including those who have a romantic interest in one another. Sometimes this is good; sometimes, it's not so good.

A well-to-do couple, acquaintances of mine from New England, were on the verge of getting married—that is, until the young fellow's mother got into the act.

In telling his fiancee about the impression she had made on his mother during a recent visit, the man said, "I'm afraid Mother thinks you're a bit crude."

"Crude?" the girl replied, greatly surprised. "Did you tell her my family traces its ancestry back to the Mayflower?"

"Why, yes."

"And did you tell her that I went to an exclusive finishing school in Paris?"

Yes, he had told her that, too.

"And did you tell her my coming-out was the high point of the social season at Newport last year?"

"Yes."

"Well," said the girl indignantly, "what's all this crude crap, then?"

Mistaken Identity

Adapting to changing social conventions can put people in ticklish situations. I was chatting with one chivalrous middle-aged man at a rather sedate party, when he indicated that he had to go upstairs to use the bathroom. Later in the evening, he regaled me with a tale that I'm still not sure I believe. It seems he walked into the bathroom to find himself standing face-to-face, so to speak, with a totally nude, voluptuous redhead.

Thinking fast, he muttered, "Excuse me, sir!" and closed the door. The woman, he felt sure, would be relieved to think that he had gotten such a brief look at her.

Later, he was sipping a drink downstairs when the redhead approached him. Expecting her to pretend not to know him—just as he planned to pretend not to know her—he opened his mouth to utter some pleasantry.

Before he could speak, she nailed him: "What the hell do you mean, calling me 'sir!' "

First-Night Jitters

We may think we live in an era of total sexual liberation, but believe it or not, there are still some old-fashioned women around. One friend told me about a young woman from a small Ohio town who had a reputation for being so innocent that most of the guys expected her not to know what to do on her wedding night.

Contrary to all expectations, however, the young woman seemed to blossom immediately after her marriage. Their friends were so impressed that the woman was invited to give a serious talk to her women's group at church about sex and married life, as seen through the eyes of a newlywed. She agreed, but she was still too embarrassed to tell her husband. When he asked about the meeting, she just said, "It's about sailing, honey" —something they had learned on their honeymoon.

A few days after the meeting, the young husband met one of the women from the church on the street. "How was my wife's talk received?" he asked the woman.

"Oh, she was excellent," the woman said. "She really seems to be well informed."

"Isn't that strange?" the husband said. "Do you know the first time she tried it, she lost her shoes, her hat blew off, and she got sick to her stomach!"

Sexy Senior

Older folks can certainly enjoy the company of the opposite sex. The encounters may be less frequent and less intense, but the waters of older love and passion often run deep—and sometimes are surprisingly turbulent.

A policeman I encountered on one of my trips to Indiana told me about a little old lady who came into his stationhouse a while ago. She told the sergeant on duty that she had been molested, and the cop asked for details.

"A man grabbed me as I was walking across the park," she said. "He pulled me behind some bushes and started kissing me and making mad, passionate love."

"And what did this assailant look like?" the sergeant asked, busily filling out a report.

"He was about six feet tall," she said, "with broad shoulders, curly black hair and dark blue eyes."

"And when did this assault take place?" the sergeant asked.

"Fifty-three years ago," she said.

"Fifty-three years ago! And you're just now reporting it?" said the puzzled sergeant.

"Oh, I'm not reporting it," the little old lady explained hastily. "I just like to come in now and then and *talk* about it."

Semper Fidelis

A Southern gentleman I know volunteered for service as a marine in South Vietnam during the Vietnam war. His new wife, meanwhile, decided to spend the year in Japan so that they could be together when her husband had leave.

The young fellow trusted his bride implicitly—that is, until he began to receive letters from her referring to all the nice guys she was meeting in Tokyo.

He finally got so upset that he arranged a radio hookup to talk directly to his wife to find out what was going on. When her voice came on the line, he could barely contain his anger.

"Hey, what exactly is happening up there?"

"Why, what on earth are you talking about, dear?" she replied sweetly.

"I'm talking about all those guys you say you're having drinks with and seeing every night!"

"Why honey," she said, "they're just target practice until the real action begins again!"

Lovebirds

The Red Light Weight Reduction Program

The owner of a certain red-light establishment was able to avoid trouble with the law because she billed the services as a weight-reduction program.

Upon signing in, the "client" was offered a five-, ten-, fifteen-, or twenty-five-pound weight-loss program. One overweight friend of mine reasoned that one way or the other, he was sure to get his money's worth.

So he paid his $5.00, and was introduced to a very attractive blonde. On her back was a sign that said, "If you catch me, you can have me."

Well, she ran all over the place, with my friend huffing and puffing behind her. She finally ran into the bedroom, and after they had spent some time together, he weighed himself. Sure enough, he'd lost five pounds.

The next week, he came back for the ten-pound program. They sent him to a room, and this time, there was an even more voluptuous, full-bodied brunette, with another sign, "If you can catch me, you can have me."

Once again, he ran himself ragged—up and down stairs, outside around the back yard, even under the porch. He got on the scale afterwards, and to his amazement, his weight had dropped ten pounds.

The next week, he decided to go for broke.

"I want to lose twenty-five pounds," he demanded.

So, they sent him to another room, and inside there was an enormous, hairy gorilla. On its back was a sign, "If I catch you, I can have you."

Making Comparisons

Some people can't shake the doubt of their spouse's faithfulness. Sometimes, the feeling seems to be that once a woman has had a taste of sex, she will never be satisfied. One person I know put it this way: "I have met women who have had many love affairs, and I have met women who have never had an affair. But it is very rare to meet a woman who has had only one love affair."

The English have a saying that puts it a bit more crudely: "A slice off a cut loaf is never missed."

One of the reasons men are so suspicious, I'm sure, is that we're so insecure about whether we are attractive or successful enough.

"I'm not rich, like Sam Watson," a young man said to his lover, "and I don't drive an expensive sports car like Sam Watson, or eat at expensive restaurants, like Sam Watson. But I do love you truly."

"Oh, and I love you too," said his girlfriend. "But tell me: Who is this Sam Watson?"

Good Knight

Men are so unsettled by all this that throughout history they have gone to great lengths to ensure their wives' fidelity. In fact, that may be how contraptions like chastity belts came into being. Over lunch one day at the NBC commissary, a friend told me that throughout the history of his family, even the noblest efforts had backfired.

It seems one of his revered ancestors, a Sir Geoffrey, was going away on a crusade, and he did not entirely trust his wife.

So he locked her in the north tower of his castle. Then, he sought out his friend, Sir Reginald, and told him what he had done, and why.

"You are my oldest and most trusted friend," he explained. "So I'm leaving the key with you. If I'm not back in three years, you may set her free."

Sir Reginald accepted this solemn commission, and Sir Geoffrey mounted up and rode away. He had not traveled many miles, however, when he heard someone calling his name from the rear. Looking back, he could see in the distance a horseman approaching at a full gallop. It was Sir Reginald.

"What's the trouble?" Sir Geoffrey asked anxiously.

Panting for breath, Sir Reginald explained, "You gave me the wrong key!"

High Stakes Rummy

Where I come from, a man who was caught fooling around with another man's wife would be shot on the spot. These days, however, it's almost regarded as chic in certain circles to accept infidelity as a normal part of life. If you're caught in the act, the thing to do is to sit down and "communicate" about your "relationship."

When my friend Al came home one day to find his best friend making love to his wife, he displayed his own version of this sort of more "civilized" reaction.

His friend, still lying in bed next to the guilty spouse, said, "Look, let's be mature and reasonable adults about this situation. I'm in love with your wife, and she loves me. So, here's what I suggest: Let's play a game of gin rummy. If you win, I promise you, I won't see her again. If I win, you divorce her, and she'll be mine. What do you say?"

After a few minutes' thought, Al said, "Okay, I agree." He paused, and then added, "But to make it interesting, what do you say we play for a penny a point?"

Morning Madness

I don't know about you, but I've found that an occasional, knock-down, drag-out argument is good for a relationship. The grand-parents of a Manhattan woman who lives across the street from me bought an old farmhouse in upstate New York, but even that idyllic scene was not sufficient to defuse their periodic displays of marital fireworks. When the whole family got together for weekends in the country, they learned to expect an especially volatile routine.

Every morning, Grandpa would be the last one downstairs for breakfast, the granddaughter says. Invariably, the grand-mother would give him an exasperated look and ask him what he wanted for breakfast.

Actually, the question was unnecessary: The old fellow ate the same breakfast every day of his life—two fried eggs and a couple of slices of bacon. But still, old "Nana" would ask him every morning with a certain edge in her voice, "What do you want for breakfast?"

"Two fried eggs and some bacon!" Grandpa would reply testily.

Then Nana would raise her eyebrows with a kind of sur-prised look, and in an incredulous tone would say, "*Two* eggs?"

She always acted as though there were something particu-larly low class about having two eggs for breakfast. As soon as she said that, the fight would be on. Grandpa would bang on the table and start cursing and yelling something about two eggs.

And Nana would get haughtier and haughtier and remind her spouse not to use such bad language in front of the children and grandchildren. Finally, Nana would cook him the two eggs, and the fight would be forgotten—at least until the next morning, when it would start all over again.

This went on for years, but then as the couple grew older, they started coming down to a grandson's home in Brooklyn to spend some time during the winter months. Unfortunately, though, when they stayed there, the cooking would always be done for them, and they really didn't have any excuse to lock horns. After a few visits, however, the grandchildren began to notice something strange: Nana and Grandpa began to spend part of their mornings down in the basement, where they raised their voices arguing with one another. The grandson's wife got upset and worried about these battles. But he just laughed and said, "They *need* their morning argument! It gets their blood stirred up for the day."

Interestingly, Grandpa didn't live very long after Nana died, probably in part because he couldn't find anyone else who could keep him primed with a good verbal donnybrook.

Meeting Your Match

Sometimes arguments can chip away at a relationship and even destroy it. One group of married couples were sitting in front of a fire enjoying a nice quiet evening with one another. The subject got around to the circumstances under which the couples had met. Finally, one woman, who had been drinking too much and seemed to be embarrassing her husband, turned to him and asked coyly, "Who introduced us, sweetie?"

The man promptly came back with, "We just happened to meet. I can't blame anybody."

Like Father, Like Son

Often the beginning of the end of a relationship may be signaled with behind-the-back criticisms. One second grade teacher had to call in little Conrad's mother for a conference.

"Your little Conrad is an extremely bright little boy for his age, Mrs. Jackson," the teacher said. "But I'm afraid he wants to spend all of his time with the little girls, and I'm trying to break him of that."

"If you do, please let me know how you do it," Mrs. Jackson replied. "His father has the same habit, and I've been trying to break him for years."

Talking Trouble

Sometimes, of course, it's the wife who is the offender. For instance, I was once introduced to a man who said he was involved in a divorce suit for cruelty. Unfortunately, he had found himself face to face with a judge who seemed to have little sympathy for his side of the story.

"I understand, sir," said the judge in addressing the husband, "that one of the indignities you have showered upon your wife is that you have not spoken to her for three years. Is that so?"

"It is, your honor," the man replied.

"Well, sir," thundered the judge, "why *didn't* you speak to her, may I ask?"

"Simply," the man said, "because I didn't want to interrupt her."

Three Strikes and You're Out

One unusual solution to the problem of the spouse who talks too much is reflected in the classic illustration of the man and wife who were traveling down the road in a mule-drawn wagon. The man, who had been fighting with his mule for years, was not in any mood for funny business. But after the wagon had been rattling down the road for a short time, the mule kicked up his heels and stumbled. "That's one!" the husband said.

The wagon finally got rolling, but in a little while, the mule kicked and stumbled again. "That's two!" the husband said.

The wagon went on again for a little distance, and then the mule kicked and stumbled once more and the wagon almost tipped over. "That's three!" the man screamed, and he snatched up his rifle, aimed it at the animal, and shot him dead.

With that, his wife decided she had gone through enough. "What did you do a stupid thing like that for? You and your fool temper! What are you going to do now?"

The man looked up at her and said quietly, "That's one."

My Mary has never treated me quite like this mule. But I'm still waiting for that day when she says, "That's one!"

XII

HAIR RAISERS

his may be the shortest section of the book, but that's only appropriate because I've been short-changed in the hair department. When I was nineteen, my hairline had already started to "recede," and by the time I was twenty-five I had a dome you could buff.

It must have been my sense of the absurd that led me into the one line of work where being bald can be a major drawback. It might be because, with all the bright lights on a television production set, the glare reflecting off the top of a bald head would send the camera people crazy trying to maintain proper contrast. When I asked my producer about this complex technical problem, he just had one suggestion: "Willard, put on a wig."

WILLARD SCOTT'S DOWN HOME STORIES

Hair Debut

The first time I ever wore hair on television was for a lobster commercial. I was to do the commercial live, breaking for a minute from my regular duties on the show. But the company refused to hire me unless I agreed to wear a hairpiece. I guess they had some strange concerns about how a bald man could adversely affect the product's image. Lobsters are hardly the hairiest animals on earth so I didn't quite see the connection. It would've made more sense to me if they'd asked me to get a nice, bright sunburn to match my co-star's coloration, but it was, in truth, a case of "hair today or gone tomorrow."

Naturally, I was extremely self-conscious, because viewers would see me bald one minute—in full, glossy bloom—and then, when the commercial suddenly flipped on, they'd think I was pitching fertilizer. As it happened, my hair was the last thing I should have worried about.

During the commercial, I was supposed to hold up the lobsters with their claws waving all about demonstrating their friskiness and my bravery. But ten minutes before I was sup- posed to do this commercial, the lobsters arrived—DOA. To save the day, they put little pieces of black thread on the lobster claws and the stage manager stood over the lobsters and me with a ladder, working the lobster like a puppet.

Roots of Fame

Wigs can look awfully phony sometimes. You can walk down the street and say, "That's the best hairpiece I ever saw," but you *can* still see it. Obviously you shouldn't be able to detect the very best ones. But even the best can look worse than natural locks. Part of the problem is that hairpieces look the same every single day, unlike natural hair, which grows and gets shaggy.

John Cameron Swayze had this problem licked as well as anyone I ever heard. He didn't just have a hairpiece—he had three or four! One would be cut just like a fresh haircut, all neat and trim. He would wear that for a few days, and then he would replace that with a second hairpiece that was a shade longer. Each successive hairpiece got longer and shaggier, until at the end of a few weeks it looked as if he needed a haircut—and he'd put the first one on again!

National Hairlines

Hairpieces are inherently kind of funny—putting one on for the first time gives you a nagging, unnatural feeling, as if you're Astroturfing the North 40 or something. Wearing one takes some getting used to. A decent one has to be custom-made to fit your scalp; no small technological feat, I assure you. At my first fitting they sat me down in a barber chair, leaning it way back to prevent my escape, and tried to determine from some old pictures what my original hairline used to look like. Then an artist put a piece of plastic over my head, and he drew in where he thought the hairline and the part should go. Finally he simply lifted off the plastic and went to work, cutting a rug, so to speak.

At first I was a little embarrassed about wearing it. I always wondered if people would notice and what they would think about it. But I've come full circle now.

First of all, I began to get bold about "exposing myself" when I was a weatherman in Washington. In fact, we made it a kind of local tradition on New Year's Eve to all get dressed up in tuxedos for our late night news broadcast. At the end of the show, I would bow to the television camera and rip off my toupee, and on the top of my bald skull I had written "Happy New Year!" I loved to "let my hair down" once in a while.

I'm never quite sure what I'm going to do when I'm feeling particularly crazy, or when the hairpiece starts to itch a little. During an appearance I made on Tom Snyder's television show, right in the middle of the interview I told him that I had a gift for him. He had no idea what I was up to, and he glanced behind the cameras to see if he was going to get a pie in the face or something. I guess he knows I'm a serious sort of person.

Well, he was never prepared for what followed. Right on national television I ripped off my hairpiece and plopped it on his desk. Then I wished him the best of luck and walked off. I think it was the first time I ever saw Tom Snyder speechless.

Government Flypaper

Sticking the hairpiece onto your scalp can be a messy business. Most hairpieces are attached to the scalp in one of two ways: On some, there are little plastic points underneath the hairpiece where you attach glue or some other kind of strong adhesive. (I don't recommend tar for this.) On others, like mine, you actually use sticky spirit gum to attach the fine-lace front to your scalp. The finer the lace, the less detectable the hairline, so if you've got really fine lace, it'll almost blend in with your skin. Then, you just sort of mop with a damp cloth to take the shine away from the glue.

Sometimes, though, when it's really hot, you *do* start to perspire under that mop. If you've used that sticky spirit gum to cement the hair to your head, it may even start to get a little tacky. Sometimes the gum will even streak a little down your forehead as you perspire. A congressman friend of mine used to have this same problem with his hairpiece all the time when he was at receptions. I always used to tell him I knew how long he had been at a party by the number of bugs that were stuck to his forehead.

Button Snafu

Representative William Clinger of Pennsylvania confided to me that one of his most embarrassing moments had to do with hair. He was on his way to a political rally, shaking hands all around the rather large crowd. He reached over the head of an elderly woman to grasp the hand of someone behind her, and his cuff button got tangled in the woman's hair. As he pulled his hand back, with it came the woman's coiffure, perky little hair ornaments and all. Clinger certainly lived up to his name the day he literally pulled the wool over his constituent's eyes!

Man's Best Friend

One time, I got a really bad hairpiece. To call it a rug would be a gross understatement—a throw rug might be more like it. I mean, this one was *raunchy*. I only keep one hairpiece, because they can get awfully expensive. So imagine my dread when I remembered that fifty guests were expected for a party at my home that night—and me looking like a family of swallows were nesting on my head.

I knew it was bad, but I didn't realize just how bad until I got home. As I walked up the steps to the house, the dog came running up to greet me, yipping a little and wagging his tail. But as soon as he caught sight of my face—and the strange contraption on my head—he just stopped dead and looked at me in a funny way. He cocked his head, and gave a kind of low growl. I guess you just don't know who your true friends are until you've hit bottom.

I got back at him later, though, when all our guests came: I made the dog wear that lousy hairpiece the rest of the evening. And I threw it away soon after. Any hairpiece that can stop a dog dead in his tracks just isn't fit for public viewing.

The Hairjacking

In Washington, I kept my hair in a drawer in the newsroom right next to my weather books. (It's not so strange. After all, how many people keep their teeth in a glass.) I didn't want to wear it all the time, and I didn't want to carry it around with me like a pet Pekinese either. This way, I could come in ten minutes before going on the air, dab on the glue, and have every costly hair in place by air time.

One day I came in for the regular five o'clock broadcast, and I sat down at my desk with eight minutes until air time. When I opened the drawer, though, my hair was gone! I rummaged from one drawer to the next, thinking that I had just misplaced it.

Actually, one of the women who worked in the newsroom had hidden the hair as a gag, and although she meant to tell me about it, she became preoccupied and forgot.

Well, with ten seconds to air time, there was nothing I could do, so I went on the air that night without the hairpiece. The producers almost croaked. It caused an enormous furor, and I announced with a straight face over the air that some dirty dog, some real low-life, had stolen my hair. We made such a hilariously big deal about the theft of my hair that what could have been a disaster turned into the best ratings of the season the following night. Everyone in town must have tuned in for the six o'clock news to see if Willard got his hair back.

Airplane Fright

Having completed an Old Farmer's Almanac interview in New Hampshire, I immediately rushed to the airport to catch my plane back to New York.

I was too late to check my bags, so I had to carry everything on the plane with me. But they didn't have electronic detectors at this airport, so a pleasant, smiling young woman took my luggage piece by piece and opened each one. She matter-of-factly opened my hairpiece box, but when she looked inside, she blanched and screamed!

The whole airport must have come running to see what was wrong, and they looked at me accusingly.

"Well," I said, "she was getting into my hair."

Tarantula Tresses

An NBC cameraman I worked with for a time had a wonderful hairpiece, but he always had trouble with the adhesive that makes it stick. While on an assignment in Mexico City, he took a break in the afternoon with a lovely señorita he had met and they decided to repair to his hotel room to avoid the heat of the day.

One thing led to another, and soon they were creating their own kind of heat, passionately embracing each other. In the middle of their lovemaking, however, his hairpiece fell off. The señorita didn't realize it, and she placed her hand right where it had fallen on the bed. The next thing he knew, his amour was running out of the room, screaming, "A tarantula!"

XIII

WAR STORIES

t times we all may live through what seems our civilization's darkest hours. Still, there will always be something that sticks out in our minds as being particularly funny, even when things are at their lowest ebb.

Serving in the military is rarely viewed as a funny experience. But my own time in uniform was really not bad at all. I was in the Navy between 1956 and 1958, and the only sea duty I had was during peacetime. My assignment was with the Supreme Allied Command Atlantic—NATO headquarters in the United States.

I think my greatest contribution to the Navy during those two years was that I helped the admiral's wife write a cookbook. Because I had some experience in show business, she came to me with all these recipes and ideas, intent upon getting it published. So she put together the book, and I did my bit to help her promote it. Somehow, I even arranged for her to get on the "Today" show—way back when they didn't know who I was.

By far, my least favorite times in the service were at basic training. I just hated the isolation and the constant drilling. While nobody escapes doing guard duty at the camp, I was unlucky enough to draw the midnight to 4:00 a.m. shift. I tell you, they really know how to give a guy responsibility. My area to "guard with my life" in the dead of night included the clothes-line and the garbage dumpster! After a couple of hours of this boring stuff, I just said the heck with it, and retired to the dumpster. It may sound disgusting, but it smelled better than those sweaty barracks!

Despite such problems, I was able to win a few favors during that time at boot camp from our section chief. He used to love to listen to the Grand Ol' Opry on Saturday night, but the reception was so terrible, he couldn't get it on his radio. So, using my limited technical knowledge of radio, I hooked up a clothes hanger and wire to his set, and sure enough, we picked up every last twang of those Nashville sounds. The chief was so grateful, he used to sneak me out of camp in the trunk of his car once in a while, so I could get a beer in town.

My relationships with my superiors weren't always so cordial, however. One day while doing sea duty, I was scraping paint on the deck of a destroyer with a fellow sailor. It was hot, dirty work, and we were trying to make the best of it by talking and joking a bit.

But we had an officer who didn't appreciate good humor. The meanest creature I ever ran across while in the Navy— including most shark and piranha—he just wouldn't have any talking among his men. He came right up to us, screaming, "Hey, stop shooting the crap!"

I looked straight at the officer, pointed my finger and said, "Bang, Bang."

Fortunately, he elected not to court-martial me for disrespect—or maybe assault with a deadly weapon.

On balance, though, my memories of the Navy are that it was a time when I had some terrific adventures—and a time when I made some wonderful friends. Few people can say they enjoyed their time in the service, but in fact, I loved it. I guess part of the reason was that I got a chance to travel. Having had some on-the-air experience, I was selected to do a five-minute radio show. At one point, I was also sent to Guantanamo Bay, where I did my first weather piece for television.

Why they put me on the tube to do the weather, I'll never know. I'd never done weather in my life. I spent most of my time in the Navy as a deckhand, doing all the dirty work. I was scraping, painting, all that good stuff. Maybe they heard me saying one day, with my deep voice, how much I loved that type of work—and then they decided that with that voice, I should be on the air. I couldn't have agreed more—I'd have done anything to get away from chores like scraping paint.

Ever since that baptism into the world of television weather, I've had a fond spot in my heart for the military and have always been willing to pay the service a friendly visit.

Ford Island Memories

While doing an interview for the "Today" show in Hawaii recently, I found out a little known fact: Pearl Harbor is located at a place in Hawaii known as Ford Island. That's where all those ships were docked that fateful day when the Japanese launched their attack.

While in Hawaii I was privileged to interview one of the survivors of that attack—a former crewman on the U.S.S. *Oklahoma.* As we stood by the waters of Pearl Harbor, the man told me that even during that horrible moment in our history, there were some disconcerting humorous incidents. This man had one unbelievable story:

Apparently, his friend had been a steward on the ship. On shore leave the night before the attack, this steward had gotten awfully drunk. The shore patrol had snatched him up from some bar on the island, and had returned him to his ship by around six o'clock on the morning of December 7. He had completely passed out, so the shore patrol just threw him in his bunk.

Well, the Japanese attacked soon after, and as we all know, they devastated the harbor and the many ships that were anchored there. After the attack was over, navy personnel swarmed onto the burning hulks of ships to rescue what they could. Through the smoke and the fire, they found this guy on the bunk and put him on a stretcher they were using to remove the dead and seriously wounded.

As they were carting him off, the inebriated steward woke up, with words that will live on forever: "What happened?" This guy had slept through the whole thing and never got a single scratch!

That's the type of story that will be told at reunions of these soldiers for years to come.

Sentry's Stammer

During the Revolutionary War, the Continental Army drafted some men from their local militias. One captain, who had just rounded up some new "recruits," asked if any of them had objections.

"I ca-ca-ca-ca-can't go," said one young soldier, "because I st-st-st-stutter."

"Stutter!" exclaimed the captain. "You don't go there to talk, but to fight."

"A-a-a-a-aye," said the young soldier, "but they'll p-p-p-put me on g-g-g-g-guard duty, and I'll be t-t-t-taken and run through the g-g-g-guts before I can cry, "W-w-who g-g-goes th-th-there.""*

Best of Enemies

Shortly after D-Day, in 1944, General Eisenhower paid a visit to a field hospital. In one of the beds he found a soldier, a veteran I encountered much later who at the time was far and away the most battle-scarred man Eisenhower had ever seen. The man was literally swathed in bloody bandages. From head to foot, he was a mass of cuts and bruises. He had a severe concussion. Both legs were broken and in traction, as was one arm.

"Son," said Eisenhower, "what in the world happened to you?"

"I was in a foxhole by the side of a road," the young man groaned, "and a German soldier was in a foxhole on the other side of the road. We shot at each other until we both ran out of ammunition. Then, he stood up and yelled, 'Roosevelt is a dummkopf!' I stood up and yelled back, 'Hitler is a jerk!' And while we were standing in the road, shaking hands, a tank ran over us."

---

* From TAR HEEL LAUGHTER by Richard Walser. Copyright The University of North Carolina Press 1974. Used with permission of the publisher.

Military Precision

Back home, a story still circulates about a young soldier whose duty it was to fire a cannon in the fort every afternoon at five o'clock sharp. To make sure he had the correct time, he always stopped at a bakery in the village and set his watch by a battered old alarm clock the baker kept in the window. Then he would proceed on to the fort and fire the cannon.

In time, the young soldier came to marvel at the accuracy of the old clock. Every day, rain or shine, he set his watch by it, and it was always right to the second.

One day, his curiosity got the better of him and he went in and talked to the baker. "Your clock is a remarkable timepiece," he said. "Every day I check my watch against it, and it always has the correct time."

"It should," the baker replied. "I set it every afternoon at five o'clock by the cannon up at the fort."

Plodding Pilot

As much as I like the military, I must say I have always noticed a tendency for the service to be long on red tape. You know the old expression "SNAFU"—well the military has always been that way. During World War II, a pilot was ordered to fly over Germany with a load of propaganda leaflets. Three months passed and he didn't return. The other pilots in his squadron were sure he had been shot down and taken prisoner, or worse—killed. So they were all greatly surprised when he finally turned up one day.

His commanding officer was puzzled. "Do you mean to tell me it has taken you three months to drop a load of propaganda leaflets?" he asked.

"Drop them?" said the pilot. "I've been going along slipping them under doors."

Besting the Blitz

In peacetime or wartime, a stint in the service almost always inspires romance. I know I considered myself something of a dashing Don Juan in uniform, even though I did more posturing than acting with the ladies. But colleagues I know who actually came under fire said that the presence of dangers could trigger more explosive passions.

During the Blitz of London, for example, an air raid warden went down in a subway tunnel to check on the people who were taking shelter there. "Are there any expectant mothers down there?" he called.

A few moments later, a young girl called back, "Not yet. We've only been down here a few minutes."

Landlocked Marine

I have several friends who were marines, but frankly, the tough training always seemed a little uncivilized to me. When I was in the Navy, we worked with marines, and I'll never forget one group of young jarhead recruits who were undergoing a course in combat swimming. The program included jumping into a pool from a twelve-foot-high diving board.

One of the recruits walked tentatively out to the end of the board, but he froze there, and could not jump.

"You had better jump, boy!" his drill instructor ordered. But the fellow still hesitated.

"What would you do," the drill instructor yelled, "if that diving board was a sinking ship?"

"Sir," the unnerved recruit yelled back, "I'd wait until it sank about ten more feet."

True Feelings

Hitler caught it from every angle when I was growing up during the war. There was a story we told and retold that went like this:

With the Allies pounding Germany day and night, Hitler wanted to find out how the people really felt about him. So one night, he slipped on a disguise and went to a movie theater in Berlin.

A newsreel came on that showed some pictures of the Führer himself, to which the entire audience reacted by jumping up and giving the stiff-armed Nazi salute and shouting, "Heil Hitler!"

Hitler was so overcome by this display of loyalty and affection that he didn't think to stand up himself. Then, a man behind him tapped him on the shoulder and said softly, "We all feel the same way about the s.o.b., my friend, but you'd better stand up, anyway. Otherwise, you'll get in trouble with the Gestapo."

Cunning Prisoner

World War I had its share of heroes, and the famous German fighter pilot, The Red Baron—another of my heroes, even though he was on the wrong side—was one of the most illustrious. He was legendary for his toughness and imperviousness to pain, and I guess that's why I'm drawn to him. You see, I'm such a softy, I can hardly stand a pinprick.

Anyhow, it seems that the Baron was shot down over the British lines, and, according to this story, he was taken prisoner. The next day, the British pilot who had shot him down visited him in the hospital.

"Is there anything you want?" the British pilot asked his famous prisoner.

"Yes, there is," the Baron replied. "They had to amputate my right arm. Would you take it and drop it over the German lines?"

Grisly though the task was, the pilot agreed to do it. A few days later, he went to see the Baron again.

"The doctors have amputated my left leg," said the Baron. "Would you mind dropping it behind German lines?"

Once again, the British pilot agreed to the gruesome task, and he went back to see the Baron again. And as before, the Baron had another request: "They've amputated my right leg, as well," he said. "Do you think you could drop it behind the German lines?"

"I can do it, of course," said the British pilot, "But, look here, Baron, you aren't trying to escape, are you?"

XIV

HOME SWEET HUMOR

here is tremendous power in humor. A funny or fascinating down-home story or saying can add flavor to life like nothing else I know. A good laugh is the best mediator for settling disputes. A smile that follows a good yarn wins friends in a flash and can influence an entire roomful of total strangers.

It's been proven to me time and time again whenever I travel across this great land, that a sense of humor is our greatest unifying force. I can meet crowds of people for the first time in my life, swap a few funny stories, and I feel like I walk out of the room with fifty or a hundred new friends.

You might call me an optimist or a romantic at heart, but I believe that if you look hard enough for the bright side of any situation, you're sure to find it. Of course, I am the type of person who still believes in Santa Claus, the Easter Bunny, and the Tooth Fairy. I mention this as a point of information, not as an apology. I'm aggressive, and you might even say militant, about the value of clean, wide-eyed fantasy.

The spirit behind my simple beliefs is what makes me tick. Some people refer to it as a childlike quality, and that suits me just fine. Like a child, I can daydream and allow my imagination to be stimulated. I can express wonder about all sorts of curious things. I can get as wrapped up in a Walt Disney film as I can in a good book, all because I can believe in what's happening on the screen, and I can let my imagination take me away.

That's why I like the stories that are handed down from generation to generation, whether short, funny tales or longer pearls of Americana like the Legend of Sleepy Hollow and Johnny Appleseed. I feel quite free to imagine that these things really happened, and to wonder at what the world in those by-gone days must have been like.

The art of using this imagination is what makes story-telling come alive for me. As long as I can insert myself into a story and maybe add a little personal touch, I'm satisfied. I enjoy sharing personal experiences that show that my own world is a truly funny place in which to live—and we're a strange but lovable lot who inhabit it.

More than any other kind of emotion, laughter is a special kind of release for me. I look forward to times when I can interact with a group of people, join in and let out a good belly laugh, and share the funny experiences of friends and neighbors.

As you've seen in the foregoing pages, stories told by our nation's political leaders also have a special meaning for me. I really identify with politicians because I think we're a lot alike: For one thing, we both depend on the approval of the masses of people. Without popular approval, TV weathermen and senators both bite the dust.

Politicians come from the most varied backgrounds imaginable, and they've met scores of off-beat people along the way.

It's a politician's job to practice the art of "getting along," and to find that area of commonality among a wide variety of people. It always tickles me to hear a politician tell stories that ring so true that they could be about my next door neighbor. As big a country as this is, we're really not so far apart from each other after all.

Finally, the stories passed down by the older folks may be those that can light up my day the most. I know that the fact that a person has lived a long time certainly doesn't mean he's automatically a sage. But it's been a privilege for me to meet so many of our older citizens who *are* wise beyond their many years, and to share those moments in their lives that make living any life worthwhile.

The old and young alike throughout our land have so much to tell and teach, I just hope that I can remember half the stories I've heard. Then, if I get to a grand old age myself, you can count on one thing: I'll pass the best of those stories down to the next generation and entrust them with the down-home tradition that has added so much light and laughter to my own life.

Now, let's part ways with a smile, and with our minds full of these words from Ralph Waldo Emerson, which are my favorites on the subject of good humor and great wisdom:

"To laugh often and much:

to win the respect of intelligent people and the affection of children,

to earn the appreciation of honest critics and endure the betrayal of false friends,

to appreciate beauty,

to find the best in others,

to leave the world a bit better whether by a healthy child, a garden patch, or a redeemed social condition;

to know even one life has breathed easier because you lived.

This is to have succeeded."